Fortieth Edition

THE 2016 CALIFORNIA NOTARY LAW PRIMER

All the hard-to-find information every California Notary Public needs to know!

National Notary Association

Published by:

National Notary Association
9350 De Soto Avenue
Chatsworth, CA 91311-4926
(800) 876-6827
Fax: (818) 700-0920
Website: www.NationalNotary.org
Email: nna@NationalNotary.org

©2015 National Notary Association
ALL RIGHTS RESERVED. No part of this book may be reproduced in any form without permission in writing from the publisher.

The information in this *Primer* is correct and current at the time of its publication, although new laws, regulations and rulings may subsequently affect the validity of certain sections. This information is provided to aid comprehension of state Notary Public requirements and should not be construed as legal advice. Please consult an attorney for inquiries relating to legal matters.

Fortieth Edition ©2015
First Edition ©1978

ISBN: 978-1-59767-190-3

Table of Contents

Introduction 1

Notary Laws Explained 2

    The Notary Commission 2

    Official Notarial Acts 10

    Practices and Procedures 25

    Misconduct, Fines and Penalties 60

California Laws Pertaining to Notaries Public 70

Documents Affecting Real Property 110

About the NNA 114

Index 115

Have a Tough Notary Question?

If you were a National Notary Association member, you could get the answer to that difficult question. Join the NNA® and your membership includes access to the NNA® Hotline* and live Notary experts providing the latest Notary information regarding laws, rules and regulations.

Hours
Monday – Friday   5:00 a.m.–7:00 p.m. (PT)
Saturday   5:00 a.m.–5:00 p.m. (PT)

NNA® Hotline Toll-Free Phone Number: 1-888-876-0827

After hours you can leave a message or email our experts at Hotline@NationalNotary.org and they will respond the next business day.

*Access to the NNA® Hotline is for National Notary Association members and NNA® Hotline subscribers only. Call and become a member today.

Introduction

The National Notary Association commends you on your interest in California Notary law! Purchasing *The California Notary Law Primer* identifies you as a conscientious professional who takes your official duties seriously.

In few fields is the expression "more to it than meets the eye" truer than in Notary law. What often appears on the surface to be a simple procedure may, in fact, have important legal considerations.

The purpose of *The California Notary Law Primer* is to provide you with a resource to help decipher the many intricate laws that affect notarization. In so doing, the *Primer* will acquaint you with all of the important aspects of California's Notary law and with prudent notarial practices in general.

This edition of *The California Notary Law Primer* contains information about the new form of identification that California Notaries may use under satisfactory evidence.

The California Notary Law Primer takes you through the myriad of Notary laws and puts them in easy-to-understand terms. Every section of the law is analyzed and explained, as well as topics not covered by California law but nonetheless of vital concern to you as a Notary.

For handy reference, we have reprinted the complete text of the laws of California that relate to Notaries Public.

Whether you are about to be commissioned for the first time, or a longtime Notary, we are sure that *The California Notary Law Primer* will provide you with new insight and understanding.

                        Milton G. Valera
                        Chairman
                        National Notary Association

Notary Laws Explained

In layperson's language, this chapter discusses and clarifies key parts of the state laws that regulate Notaries Public. Most of these laws are reprinted in full in "California Laws Pertaining to Notaries Public" beginning on page 70.

This edition explains the recent changes to California law, including new requirements for notices on acknowledgment, jurat, and proof of execution certificates, as well as a new penalty for willful failure of duty.

Additional information about California's requirements for Notaries Public is available on the Secretary of State's website. For step-by-step instructions on the commission application process, applicants may also visit *www.nationalnotary.org/california/become-a-notary*.

THE NOTARY COMMISSION

Application for Commission

Qualifications. To become a Notary in California, the applicant must (Government Code, Sections 8201, 8201.1, 8201.2 8201.5 and 8214.1):

1) Be a legal California resident, or a federal civil servant on a military base in accordance with Government Code, Section 8203.1.

2) Be at least 18 years old.

3) Complete and pass a proctored, written examination prescribed by the Secretary of State.

4) Have fingerprints electronically scanned for a background check by the state Department of Justice (DOJ) and the Federal Bureau of Investigation (FBI) for a federal summary of criminal information.

5) Not have been convicted of a felony or of a crime involving moral turpitude.

6) Be able to read, write and understand the English language.

7) Complete a six-hour education course regarding the Notary's functions and duties. Renewing Notaries who have completed a state-approved six-hour course and whose commissions have not yet expired must complete a refresher course of at least three hours

8) Submit a 2-inch by 2-inch color passport-style photograph of his or her person.

State-Residency Requirements. To become a Notary in California, the applicant must be a legal resident of the state. State officials maintain that a legal resident is a person who demonstrates the intent to permanently reside in the state by registering to vote or by obtaining a California driver's license.

A Notary is prohibited from using a commercial mail receiving agency or post office box as a principal place of business or residence unless the applicant also provides a physical street address (Government Code, Section 8213.5).

Citizenship. U.S. citizenship is not required to become a California Notary, though any non-citizen applicant must be a legal resident. A 1984 U.S. Supreme Court decision, *Bernal v. Fainter*, declared that no state may deny a Notary commission merely based on the lack of U.S. citizenship.

Application Fee. The application fee is $40, payable at the site of the proctored exam. Applicants must also pay a $49 print processing fee plus a print-rolling fee at a "Live Scan" fingerprint scanning site. The print-rolling fees vary from location to location.

Application Misstatement. Substantial and material misstatement or omission in the application for a Notary commission is reason for the Secretary of State to revoke, suspend or refuse to grant a Notary commission (Government Code, Section 8214.1).

Delinquency on Child Support Payments. The Secretary of State is prohibited from issuing or renewing a Notary commission for any person who has not complied with child support orders. Any commission fees that have been paid by the applicant will not be refunded (Welfare and Institutions Code, Section 11350.6).

Dishonored Check. The Secretary of State may cancel the commission of a Notary Public if the commission fee is not paid due to a returned check. Upon receiving notice from a financial institution that a check or draft was not honored, the Secretary of State will notify the applicant and request payment by cashier's check. Should the Secretary of State need to issue a second notice, the commission will be cancelled effective the date of that second notice (Government Code, Section 8204.1).

Examination

Required. All Notary commission applicants — including renewing Notaries — must complete and pass a proctored, written examination prescribed by the Secretary of State.

Cooperative Personnel Services (CPS), a private organization contracted by the state, administers the proctored exam at sites throughout California. For information about taking the exam, contact CPS at (916) 263-3520. For information about taking the exam following an National Notary Association seminar, call (800) 876-6827.

State-Approved Education Course

Required. California law requires first-time Notary commission applicants to complete a state-approved six-hour course covering a Notary's functions and duties. Renewing Notaries who have completed a state-approved six-hour course and whose commissions have not yet expired must complete a refresher course of at least three hours.

Fingerprints

Applicants' Prints Electronically Scanned. Whether renewing or applying for the first time, commission applicants must have their fingerprints electronically scanned at a Live Scan site (Government Code, Section 8201.1).

Live Scan Sites. Live Scan sites are located throughout the state. To receive a list of designated sites, an applicant may contact the National Notary Association at (800) 876-6827, the Notary Section at (916) 653-3595 or Sylvan/Identix at (800) 315-4507 or obtain the list online at *www.ag.ca.gov/fingerprints/publications/contact.php*.

Applicants should call the Live Scan site in advance to determine the hours of operation and if an appointment is needed. A $49 print processing fee must be paid at the site, along with a print rolling fee that varies according to location.

Notary Bond

Requirement. California Notaries are required to obtain a bond of $15,000 and file it at the office of the county clerk in the county of their principal place of business (Government Code, Section 8212).

Filing the Bond. The bond must be filed along with the oath of office (see "Oath of Office," pages 6) within 30 calendar days from the beginning of the Notary's commission term. Notaries may file their bonds in person or by certified mail. The Notary commission does not take effect until the oath and bond are filed. The filing fee varies by county.

The county clerk forwards a copy of the Notary's oath and a certificate, which indicates that the bond was filed, to the Secretary of State. The county clerk then delivers the bond to the county recorder for recording, after which the county recorder mails a copy of the bond to the Notary. The Notary should keep the bond in a safe place for at least six years — the statutory limitation for lawsuits resulting from a notarial act — after the last notarial act performed (Government Code, Section 8213).

Surety. The surety for the Notary's bond must be an approved, state-licensed bonding company. A deposit of funds may not be made in lieu of a surety bond (Government Code, Section 8212).

Protects Public. The Notary bond protects the public, not the Notary, from a Notary's misconduct or negligence. The bond provides coverage for damages to anyone who suffers financially from a Notary's actions — intentional or not. The surety company will seek compensation from the Notary for any damages it has to pay out on the Notary's behalf. The Secretary of State is authorized to require the Notary to purchase replacement bonding if the original $15,000 bond funds are depleted by damage claims.

<u>Liable for All Damages</u>. The Notary and surety company may be sued for damages resulting from notarial misconduct. The surety is liable only up to the amount of the bond, but the Notary may be found liable for any amount of money (Government Code, Section 8214).

<u>Surety's Release from Obligation</u>. If a surety believes that a Notary is likely to perform improper notarial acts in the future, the surety can appeal to the Superior Court for release from the obligation to bond the Notary. A judge may then require proof of the Notary's ability to obtain another surety. If the Notary neglects or refuses to provide a new surety, his or her commission may be revoked (Government Code, Section 8216).

<u>Errors and Omissions Insurance</u>. Notaries may choose to purchase insurance to cover any unintentional errors or omissions they may make. Notary errors and omissions insurance provides protection for Notaries who are involved in claims or sued for damages resulting from unintentional notarial errors and omissions. In the event of a claim or civil lawsuit, the insurance company will provide and pay for the Notary's legal counsel and absorb any damages levied by a court or agreed to in a settlement, up to the policy coverage limit. Generally, errors and omissions insurance does not cover the Notary for dishonest, fraudulent or criminal acts or omissions, or for willful or intentional disregard of the law.

Oath of Office

<u>Requirement</u>. California Notaries are required to take an oath of office and file it with the county clerk in the same county as their principal place of business (Government Code, Sections 8212 and 8213).

<u>Filing the Oath</u>. The oath must be taken and filed along with the Notary bond (see "Notary Bond," pages 5–6) within 30 days from the beginning of the Notary's term. The Notary commission does not take effect until this is done. Notaries may take and file the oath in person at the county clerk's office. Or the oath may be taken before another Notary Public in the same county where it will be filed and mailed by certified mail, along with the proper filing fee, to the county clerk. Filing fees vary by county (Government Code, Section 8213).

Jurisdiction

Statewide. Notaries may perform official acts throughout the state of California but not beyond the state borders. A Notary may not witness a signing outside California and then return to the state to perform the notarization. All parts of a notarial act must be performed at the same time and place within the state (Government Code, Section 8200).

Term of Office

Four-Year Term. A Notary's term of office is four years, beginning with the date specified on the commission certificate and ending at midnight on the expiration date (Government Code, Section 8204).

Reappointment

Application for Renewal. To avoid a gap between commissions, Notaries seeking reappointment should begin the application process up to a year before the end of commission. Renewal applications will not be accepted earlier than one year before expiration. Applications are available from the National Notary Association by calling (800) 876-6827 or from Cooperative Personnel Services by calling (916) 263-3520.

Fingerprints. Notaries applying for reappointment must submit new prints at a Live Scan electronic scanning site (Government Code, Section 8201.1). (See "Fingerprints," pages 4–5.)

Commission Fees. The fee for a Notary applying for reappointment is $40, just as it is for a first-time applicant.

State-Approved Education. Renewing Notaries who have previously completed a state-approved six-hour course and whose commissions have not yet expired must complete a refresher course of at least three hours (Government Code, Section 8201).

Exam Required. All new and renewing Notaries must complete and pass a written examination prescribed by the Secretary of State. (See "Examination," page 4.)

Journal. All California Notaries must maintain a journal of notarial acts for as long as they hold a Notary Public commission (Government Code, Section 8206).

Renewing Notaries may continue recording their acts in the journal from their previous commission but should make a notation in the journal when the renewed commission begins.

Oath. The oath of office must be taken — and the Notary bond filed — within 30 days from the beginning of the Notary's new commission. The new commission does not take effect until this is done (Government Code, Section 8213).

Bond. All renewing Notaries must obtain a new $15,000 bond (Government Code, Section 8212). (See "Notary Bond," pages 5–6.)

Seal. Renewing Notaries must destroy or deface the seal from their previous commission and obtain a new seal for the new commission. The procedures are the same as if obtaining a seal for the first time. (See "Notary Seal," pages 40–44.)

Resignation

Procedure. To resign, a Notary should immediately notify the Secretary of State by certified mail, destroy or deface the Notary seal and deliver the journal within 30 days to the county clerk of the county where the Notary's bond and oath of office are filed (Government Code, Section 8209). (See "Disposition of Notarial Records," pages 36–37.)

Death of Notary

In the case of a Notary's death, his or her personal representative must notify the Secretary of State and deliver all notarial records to the county clerk of the county where the Notary's bond and oath of office are filed (Government Code, Section 8209). The Notary's representative must also destroy or deface the Notary seal (Government Code, Section 8207).

Public-Employee Notaries

Terms of Appointment. The Secretary of State may appoint and issue a Notary commission to state, county, city and public school district employees to perform notarial acts only for the agencies in which they are employed. The commission ends when employment ends, or at the end of four years, whichever comes first. The employing agency may pay the premium on the Notary's bond and the cost of other required supplies from public funds at its disposal (Government Code, Section 8202.5).

No Commission Fees. When a public employee applies for a Notary commission, a signed statement is required from an authorized representative of the agency in which the Notary's services are needed. Provided this statement is filed, no state or county appointment or filing fees need be paid (Government Code, Section 8202.5).

Notarial Fees. Any fees collected by a public-employee Notary must be turned over to the agency for which the Notary works. The agency is required to deposit these fees into the same fund from which the Notary's salary is paid (Government Code, Section 8202.5).

Change of Address

Notification. The Secretary of State must be notified by certified mail within 30 days of a change in a Notary's principal place of business or residence address (Government Code, Section 8213.5).

A Notary who willfully fails to notify the Secretary of State of a change of business or residence address is guilty of an infraction and liable for a fine of up to $500 (Government Code, Section 8213.5).

Refile Oath and Bond. Since a Notary has statewide jurisdiction and may notarize in any county, the Notary is not required to refile the oath of office and bond, even if his or her principal place of business moves to a new county. However, the Notary may elect to refile the oath of office and bond in the county of the new principal place of business. If so, then the Notary must also obtain a new official seal that reflects the change within 30 days (Government Code, Section 8213).

Change of Name

Notification Required. A Notary who changes his or her name during the term of the Notary commission must notify the Secretary of State so that the commission may be amended.

A Notary who willfully fails to notify the Secretary of State of a change of name is guilty of an infraction and liable for a fine of up to $500 (Government Code, Section 8213.6).

To amend the commission, the Notary must submit to the Secretary a change of name application, which may be downloaded from the Secretary's website at *www.sos.ca.gov/notary*.

The Secretary of State will issue an amended commission with the Notary's new name. The amended commission takes effect on the date the oath and amendment to the bond are filed with the county clerk (see "File New Oath and Bond Amendment," below). The Notary's commission term and commission number remain the same. The Notary may continue notarizing in the old name until the amended commission takes effect (Government Code, Sections 8213 and 8213.6).

File New Oath and Bond Amendment. After a change of name application is filed, the Notary must also file, within 30 days of the date the amended commission is issued, a new oath of office and an amendment to the bond. The new oath and amended bond are filed with the county clerk of the county in which the Notary's principal place of business is located. The amended commission will not take effect unless the filing is done within the 30-day period (Government Code, Section 8213).

If the address of the Notary's principal place of business was also changed in the "Application for Name Change" form, a new bond (or duplicate of the original) must be filed with the county clerk with an amendment to the bond (Government Code, Section 8213).

New Seal. Within 30 days of filing the new oath and amended bond, the Notary must obtain a new official seal that reflects the name change — and county change, if applicable (Government Code, Section 8213).

OFFICIAL NOTARIAL ACTS

Authorized Acts

Notaries may perform the following notarizations (Government Code, Section 8205):

- Acknowledgments, certifying that a signer personally appeared before the Notary, was identified by the Notary and acknowledged signing the document. (See pages 12–15.)

- Certified Copy of Notarial Record, certifying, when requested by the Secretary of State, that a copy of a requested journal entry is a true copy of that entry. (See page 16.)

- <u>Certified Copy of Power of Attorney</u>, certifying that a copy of a power of attorney document is identical to the original. (See page 16.)

- <u>Depositions</u>, certifying that the spoken words of a witness in a legal matter were accurately taken down in writing, though this act is most often done by skilled court reporters. (See pages 17–18.)

- <u>Jurats</u>, as found in affidavits and other sworn documents, certifying that the signer personally appeared before the Notary, was identified by the Notary, signed in the Notary's presence and took an oath or affirmation from the Notary. (See pages 18–20.)

- <u>Oaths and Affirmations</u>, solemn promises to a Supreme Being (oath) or on one's own personal honor (affirmation). (See pages 20–22.)

- <u>Proofs of Execution</u>, certifying that a subscribing witness personally appeared and swore to the Notary that another person, the principal, signed a document. (See pages 22–24.)

- <u>Protests</u>, certifying that a written promise to pay, such as a bill of exchange, was not honored. (See pages 24–25.)

Unauthorized Acts

<u>Certified Copies</u>. A certified copy is a duplicate of an original document that is certified as an exact reproduction. In California, a Notary is prohibited from making certified copies of anything but the Notary's own official journal or a power of attorney document (Government Code, Section 8205). (See "Certified Copies of Powers of Attorney," page 16.)

Requests for certified copies of any other document should be directed to the agency that holds the original document. For certified copies of birth, death or marriage certificates and other vital records, the person requesting the certified copy should be referred to the appropriate Bureau of Vital Statistics.

In cases where the original document is not held by an outside agency but is the personal property of the owner or holder of the document, Notaries may notarize a signed, written declaration made by the document owner and stating that a copy of the original document is a true copy. This process is commonly called "copy certification by document custodian" and may serve as an acceptable alternative to a Notary-certified copy. The receiving party determines if this alternative is acceptable. The requesting person, not the Notary, should provide the declaration and specify the notarial act to be performed if a Notary certificate is not already provided on the declaration. Notaries should be careful not to guide the process or to make any recommendations or claims concerning the legality or sufficiency of this alternative.

Weddings. Although a California Notary may issue and notarize confidential marriage certificates (see "Confidential Marriage Certificates," pages 58–59), the Notary cannot perform the actual marriage ceremony unless he or she is a religious or civil official authorized to solemnize marriages. Only Notaries in Florida, Maine, Nevada and South Carolina are empowered to perform marriages strictly by virtue of holding a Notary commission.

Acknowledgments

Purpose. Acknowledgments are one of the most common forms of notarization. Typically, they are executed on deeds and other documents that will be publicly recorded by a county recorder.

In executing an acknowledgment, a Notary certifies three things (Civil Code, Section 1185):

1) The signer *personally appeared* before the Notary on the date and in the state and county indicated on the Notary certificate. (Notarization cannot be based upon a telephone call or on a Notary's familiarity with a signature.)

2) The signer was *positively identified* by the Notary through satisfactory evidence. (See "Identifying Document Signers," pages 26–30.)

3) The signer *acknowledged* to the Notary that the signature was freely made for the purposes stated in the document. (If a document is willingly signed in the presence of the Notary, this act can serve just as well as an oral statement of acknowledgment.)

NOTARY LAWS EXPLAINED

<u>Certificate for Acknowledgment</u>. For every acknowledgment on a document that will be filed in California, regardless of whom the signer is representing, California Notaries must use the California acknowledgment wording prescribed in statute. That wording is shown below.

Effective January 1, 2015, this wording must include a notice that the Notary completing the certificate is only verifying the identity of the signer and not the truthfulness, accuracy or validity of the document. This notice must be legible, enclosed in a box, and situated above the venue on the certificate (Civil Code, Sections 1188 and 1189).

> A notary public or other officer completing this certificate verifies only the identity of the individual who signed the document to which this certificate is attached, and not the truthfulness, accuracy, or validity of that document.

State of California   )
County of _____)

On _____ before me, (here insert name and title of the officer), personally appeared _____
_____, who proved to me on the basis of satisfactory evidence to be the person(s) whose name(s) is/are subscribed to the within instrument and acknowledged to me that he/she/they executed the same in his/her/their authorized capacity(ies), and that by his/her/their signature(s) on the instrument the person(s), or the entity upon behalf of which the person(s) acted, executed the instrument.

I certify under PENALTY OF PERJURY under the laws of the State of California that the foregoing paragraph is true and correct.

  WITNESS my hand and official seal.

  Signature   (Seal)

<u>Penalty of Perjury</u>. Notaries must sign all California acknowledgment certificates under penalty of perjury (Civil Code, Section 1189).

<u>Certificate for Documents Filed Out of State</u>. A California Notary may complete an acknowledgment certificate prescribed by or used in a U.S. state or jurisdiction other than California only if the document will be filed outside of California.

However, an out-of-state certificate may not be used if it requires the Notary to make any determination or certification not allowed by California law, such as certifying a signer's particular representative capacity as attorney-in-fact, corporate officer or other status. The out-of-state certificate may refer to the capacity claimed by the signer, but the Notary may not certify that the signer does, in fact, have the authority to sign under the claimed capacity (Civil Code, Section 1189[4][c]).

Identification of Acknowledger. In an acknowledgment, the Notary must identify the signer through satisfactory evidence consisting of either credible identifying witnesses or identification documents (Civil Code, Section 1185). (See "Identifying Document Signers," pages 26–30.)

Witnessing Signature Not Required. For an acknowledgment, the document does not have to be signed in the Notary's presence. However, the signer must appear before the Notary at the time of notarization to acknowledge having signed the document.

A document may have been signed an hour before, a week before, a year before, etc. — as long as the signer appears before the Notary with the signed document at the time of notarization to acknowledge that the signature is his or her own.

Failure to Complete Acknowledgment. Failure to complete an acknowledgment at the same time that the Notary's signature and seal are affixed to the document is reason for the Secretary of State to revoke, suspend or refuse to grant a Notary's commission. In addition, a fine of up to $750 may be imposed (Government Code, Sections 8214.1 and 8214.15).

False Certificate. A Notary is liable for a civil penalty of up to $10,000 for willfully stating as true any material fact in an acknowledgment certificate that he or she knows is false. This penalty may be imposed either by the Secretary of State in an administrative hearing or by a public prosecutor in superior court (Civil Code, Section 1185[b][1][B]).

Out-of-State Acknowledgment. Acknowledgment certificates completed outside of California by Notaries of another state in accordance with the laws of that state may be recorded in California (Civil Code, Section 1189).

Terminology. In discussing acknowledgments, it is important to use proper terms. A Notary takes or executes an acknowledgment, while a document signer makes or gives an acknowledgment.

Who May Take. Within the state, Notaries and the following officials may take acknowledgments and proofs of execution in their jurisdictions (Civil Code, Section 1181):

- Clerks of superior, municipal and justice courts and clerks of boards of supervisors, counties and cities

- Court commissioners; municipal, justice court and retired judges; county counsels.

- District and city attorneys

Outside of California, but within the United States and its jurisdictions, acknowledgments and proofs of execution may be made before any of the following (Civil Code, Section 1182):

- A Notary Public

- A judge, justice or clerk of any court of record of the United States

- A commissioner appointed by the Governor or Secretary of State

- Any other authorized officer

Outside of the United States, acknowledgments and proofs may be made before the following officials (Civil Code, Section 1183):

- A Notary Public, providing that the Notary's signature is proven before a judge of a court of record where the notarization is performed, by any American diplomatic officer or authorized consular agent or by *apostille*

- A judge of a court of record, a consul, vice consul or consular agent of the U.S. in the foreign jurisdiction

- A commissioner appointed by the Governor or by the Secretary of State

Certified Copies of Powers of Attorney

Procedure. In addition to notarizing signatures on powers of attorney, Notaries may certify copies of such documents. The Notary compares the copy to the original to verify that the copy is, in fact, identical to the original power of attorney document (Government Code, Section 8205 and Probate Code, Section 4307). Ideally, the Notary should personally make the photocopy that is to be certified to ensure that the copy is identical to the original.

Certificate for Certified Copy of Power of Attorney. A certificate for a certified copy of a power of attorney must state that the Notary has examined the original power of attorney and the copy and has determined that the copy is a true and correct copy of the original power of attorney (Probate Code, Section 4307[c]). The National Notary Association recommends the following wording for Notaries certifying copies of powers of attorney:

> State of California   )
>   ) ss.
> County of _____   )
>
> On this the _____ day of _____ (month), _____ (year), I, _____ (name of Notary Public), the undersigned Notary Public, hereby certify that the attached document is a true, complete and unaltered photocopy of a power of attorney presented to me on this date by _____ (presenter's name), under Section 4307 of the California Probate Code.
>
> _____ (Signature of Notary)   (Seal of Notary)

Journal Entry. The Notary must complete a journal entry for a copy certification of a power of attorney document.

Identification of Presenter. Although not required by law, the Notary should properly identify the document presenter by the same identification standards prescribed for acknowledgments.

Copies of Notarial Records

Secretary of State Request. Upon receipt of a written request from the Secretary of State, a Notary must furnish a certified copy of the requested journal entry within the time specified in the request (Government Code, Section 8205[b][1]).

Subpoena or Court Order. A Notary must provide his or her Notary journal for examination and photocopying upon receipt of a subpoena *duces tecum* or court order. The copying must be performed in the presence of the Notary, and the Notary must certify the copies if requested (Government Code, Section 8206).

Certificate for Certified Copy of Notarial Record. California law does not provide certificate wording for Notaries issuing certified copies of journal entries. The National Notary Association recommends the following form:

State of California   )
) ss.
County of _____   )

On this the _____ day of _____ (month), _____ (year), I, _____ (name of Notary Public), the undersigned Notary Public, hereby declare that the attached reproduction of a Notary journal entry involving _____ (describe document, noting date and signer[s]) is a true and correct photocopy made from a page in my Notary journal.

_____ (Signature of Notary)   (Seal of Notary)

Depositions and Affidavits

Purpose. A deposition is a signed transcript of the signer's oral statements taken down for use in a judicial proceeding. The deposition signer is called the deponent.

An affidavit is a signed statement made under oath or affirmation by a person called an affiant, and it is used for a variety of purposes both in and out of court.

Depositions. With a deposition, both sides in a lawsuit or court case have the opportunity to cross-examine the deponent. Questions and answers are transcribed into a written statement. Used only in judicial proceedings, a deposition is then signed and sworn to or affirmed before an oath-administering official.

California Notaries have the power to take depositions — meaning, to transcribe the words spoken aloud by a deponent — but this duty is most often executed by trained and certified court reporters.

Affidavits. Affidavits are used in and out of court for a variety of purposes, from declaring losses to an insurance company to declaring U.S. citizenship before traveling to a foreign country. An affidavit is a document containing a statement voluntarily signed and sworn to or affirmed before a Notary or other official with oath-administering powers. If used in a judicial proceeding, only one side in the case need participate in the execution of the affidavit, unlike with the deposition.

Certificate for Depositions and Affidavits. Depositions and affidavits generally require jurat certificates. (See "Jurats," pages 18–20.)

Oath (Affirmation) for Depositions and Affidavits. If no other wording is prescribed in a given instance, a Notary may use the following language in administering an oath (or affirmation) for an affidavit or deposition:

> Do you solemnly swear that the statements in this document are true to the best of your knowledge and belief, so help you God?
>
> (Do you solemnly affirm that the statements in this document are true to the best of your knowledge and belief?)

Response Required. For an oath or affirmation, the affiant must respond aloud and affirmatively, with "I do," "Yes" or the like.

Jurats

Purpose. In notarizing affidavits, depositions and other forms of written verification requiring an oath or affirmation by the signer, the Notary normally executes a jurat.

The purpose of a jurat is to compel truthfulness by appealing to the signer's conscience and fear of criminal penalties for perjury. In executing a jurat, a Notary certifies four things:

1) The signer *personally appeared* before the Notary at the time of notarization on the date and in the state and county indicated. (Notarization based upon a telephone call or on familiarity with a signature is not acceptable.)

2) The signer was *positively identified* by the Notary through satisfactory evidence (see "Identifying Document Signers," pages 26–30).

3) The Notary *watched the signer sign the document* at the time of notarization.

4) The Notary *administered an oath or affirmation* to the signer.

NOTARY LAWS EXPLAINED

<u>Identification</u>. In a jurat, the Notary must identify the signer based on satisfactory evidence (Government Code, Section 8202[a]). (See "Identifying Document Signers," pages 26–30.)

<u>Certificate for a Jurat</u>. California Notaries may only use jurat wording exactly as prescribed in statute; it doesn't matter where the document will be filed. That wording is shown below.

Effective January 1, 2015, this wording must include a notice that the Notary completing the certificate is only verifying the identity of the signer and not the truthfulness, accuracy or validity of the document. This notice must be legible, enclosed in a box, and situated above the venue on the certificate (Government Code, Section 8202).

> A notary public or other officer completing this certificate verifies only the identity of the individual who signed the document to which this certificate is attached, and not the truthfulness, accuracy, or validity of that document.

State of California
County of _____

Subscribed and sworn to (or affirmed) before me on this _____ day of _____ (month), _____ (year), by _____, proved to me on the basis of satisfactory evidence to be the person(s) who appeared before me.

Signature   (Seal)

If the venue in the certificate is separated from otherwise acceptable jurat wording, the Notary should line through the venue, initial and date the correction, and write or stamp the new venue above the certificate.

<u>Verifying Age</u>. In executing a jurat on a document that includes the signer's date of birth or age and the signer's photograph or fingerprint, the Notary must verify the date of birth or age through a birth certificate, a California state driver's license or a non-driver's ID (Government Code, Section 8230).

<u>Wording for Jurat Oath (Affirmation)</u>. If not otherwise prescribed by law, a California Notary may use the following or similar words to administer an oath (or affirmation) in conjunction with a jurat:

Do you solemnly swear that the statements in this document are true to the best of your knowledge and belief, so help you God?

(Do you solemnly affirm that the statements in this document are true to the best of your knowledge and belief?)

Oath or Affirmation Not Administered. Failure to administer any oath or affirmation as required by law is reason for the Secretary of State to revoke, suspend or refuse to grant a Notary commission. In addition, a fine of up to $750 may be imposed (Government Code, Sections 8214.1 and 8214.15).

Oaths and Affirmations

Purpose. An oath is a solemn, spoken pledge to a Supreme Being. An affirmation is a solemn, spoken pledge on one's own personal honor, with no reference to a Supreme Being. Both are usually a promise of truthfulness and have the same legal effect.

In taking an oath or affirmation in an official proceeding, a person may be subject to criminal penalties for perjury should he or she fail to be truthful.

An oath or affirmation can be a full-fledged notarial act in its own right, as when giving an oath of office to a public official, or it can be part of the process of notarizing a document (e.g., executing a jurat or swearing in a credible witness).

A person who objects to taking an oath may instead be given an affirmation.

Power to Administer. California Notaries and certain other officers are authorized to administer oaths and affirmations (Code of Civil Procedure, Section 2093).

Wording for Oath (Affirmation). If state law does not dictate otherwise, a California Notary may use the following or similar words in administering an oath (or affirmation):

- Oath (Affirmation) for an affiant signing an affidavit:

    Do you solemnly swear that the statements in this document are true to the best of your knowledge and belief, so help you God?

    (Do you solemnly affirm that the statements in this document are true to the best of your knowledge and belief?)

- Oath (Affirmation) for a witness testifying in a court case (Code of Civil Procedure, Section 2094):

Do you solemnly swear that the evidence you shall give in this issue (or matter), pending between (first party) and (second party), shall be the truth, the whole truth and nothing but the truth, so help you God?

(Do you solemnly affirm that the evidence you shall give in this issue [or matter], pending between [first party] and [second party], shall be the truth, the whole truth and nothing but the truth?)

- Oath (Affirmation) for a credible identifying witness (Civil Code, Section 1185):

Do you solemnly swear that (signer) is the person named in the document; that (signer) is personally known to you; that it is your reasonable belief that the circumstances of (signer) are such that it would be very difficult or impossible for him/her to obtain another form of identification; that (signer) does not possess any of the acceptable identification documents; and that you do not have a financial interest nor are you named in the document, so help you God?

(Do you solemnly affirm that [signer] is the person named in the document; that [signer] is personally known to you; that it is your reasonable belief that the circumstances of [signer] are such that it would be very difficult or impossible for him/her to obtain another form of identification; that [signer] does not possess any of the acceptable identification documents; and that you do not have a financial interest nor are you named in the document?

- Oath (Affirmation) for a subscribing witness:

Do you solemnly swear that you personally know (name of principal signer), that (name of principal signer) is the person described in and who signed this document, that you saw (name of principal) sign this document or that he/she acknowledged to you having signed it, and that you signed the document as a witness at the request of (name of principal), so help you God?

(Do you solemnly affirm that you personally know [name of principal signer], that [name of principal signer] is the person described in and who signed on this document, that you saw [name of principal] sign this document or that he/she acknowledged to you having signed it, and that you signed the document as a witness at the request of [name of principal]?)

<u>Response Required</u>. The oath or affirmation wording must be spoken aloud, and the person taking the oath or affirmation must answer affirmatively with "I do," "Yes" or the like. A nod or grunt is not a clear and sufficient response. If a person is unable to speak, the Notary may rely upon written notes to communicate.

<u>Ceremony and Gestures</u>. To impress upon the person taking the oath or affirmation the importance of truthfulness, the Notary

is encouraged to lend a sense of ceremony and formality to the oath or affirmation. During the administration of an oath or affirmation, the Notary and the oath-taker or affirmant may raise their right hands, though this is not a legal requirement. Notaries generally have discretion to use words and gestures they feel will most compellingly appeal to the conscience of the person taking the oath or affirmation.

Oath or Affirmation Not Administered. Failure to administer any oath or affirmation as required by law is reason for the Secretary of State to revoke, suspend or refuse to grant a Notary commission. In addition, a fine of up to $750 may be imposed (Government Code, Sections 8214.1 and 8214.15).

Proof of Execution by Subscribing Witness

Purpose. In executing a proof of execution, a Notary certifies that the signature of a person who does not appear before the Notary — the principal signer — is genuine and freely made based upon the sworn testimony of another person who does appear: a subscribing (signing) witness.

Proofs of execution are used when the principal signer does not appear before a Notary. Because of their high potential for fraudulent abuse, proofs should only be used as a last resort and never merely because the principal signer prefers not to take the time to personally appear before a Notary.

In Lieu of Acknowledgment. On recordable documents, a proof of execution is usually regarded as an acceptable substitute for an acknowledgment (Civil Code, Section 1195).

Limitations. Proofs of execution may not be performed on any document requiring a Notary to obtain a thumbprint in the Notary's journal from the party signing the document, including powers of attorney, deeds, quitclaim deeds, deeds of trust, mortgages, security agreements and any other document affecting real property. (See "Journal Thumbprint Requirement," page 32, and "Documents Affecting Real Property," pages 33–34 and 110–113.) Proofs are allowed with trustee's deeds resulting from foreclosure and deeds of reconveyance (Government Code, Section 27287 and Civil Code, Section 1195).

Subscribing Witness. A subscribing witness is a person who watches a principal sign a document (or who personally takes the principal's acknowledgment) and then subscribes (signs) his or her own name on the document. This witness then personally appears before a Notary with that document and takes an oath or affirmation from the Notary to the effect that the principal did willingly sign (or acknowledge signing) the document.

The ideal subscribing witness personally knows the principal signer and has no beneficial interest in the document or transaction. It would be foolish of the Notary, for example, to rely upon the word of a subscribing witness presenting for notarization a power of attorney that names this very witness as attorney-in-fact.

<u>Oath (Affirmation) for a Subscribing Witness</u>. An acceptable oath for the subscribing witness might be:

> Do you solemnly swear that you personally know (name of principal signer), that (name of principal signer) is the person described in and who signed this document, that you saw (name of principal) sign this document or that he/she acknowledged to you having signed it, and that you signed the document as a witness at the request of (name of principal), so help you God?
>
> (Do you solemnly affirm that you personally know [name of principal signer], that [name of principal signer] is the person described in and who signed on this document, that you saw [name of principal] sign this document or that he/she acknowledged to you having signed it, and that you signed the document as a witness at the request of [name of principal]?)

The subscribing witness then signs the Notary's journal and the Notary completes a California proof of execution by subscribing witness certificate.

<u>Identifying the Subscribing Witness</u>. The subscribing witness's identity must be proved on the oath of one credible identifying witness who is personally known to the Notary. The credible witness must also present a valid state-approved ID card to the Notary (Civil Code, Section 1196).

<u>Certificate for Proof of Execution</u>. California Notaries may only use certificate wording for a proof of execution exactly as prescribed in statute. That wording is shown below.

Effective January 1, 2015, this wording must include a notice that the Notary completing the certificate is only verifying the identity of the signer and not the truthfulness, accuracy or validity of the document. This notice must be legible, enclosed in a box, and situated above the venue on the certificate (Civil Code, Section 1195).

> A notary public or other officer completing this certificate verifies only the identity of the individual who signed the document to which this certificate is attached, and not the truthfulness, accuracy, or validity of that document.

State of California) ss.
County of _____)

On _____ (date), before me _____(name and title of officer), personally appeared _____ (subscribing witness's name), proved to me to be the person whose name is subscribed to the within instrument, as a witness thereto, on the oath of _____ (name of credible witness), a credible witness who is known to me and provided a satisfactory identifying document. _____ (name of subscribing witness), being by me duly sworn, said that he/she was present and saw/heard _____ (name[s] of principal[s]), the same person(s) described in and whose name(s) is/are subscribed to the within or attached instrument in his/her/their authorized capacity(ies) as (a) party(ies) thereto, execute or acknowledge executing the same, and that said affiant subscribed his/her name to the within or attached instrument as a witness at the request of _____ (name[s] of principal[s]).

WITNESS my hand and official seal.

Signature   (Seal)

Do Not Use Acknowledgment Form. The acknowledgment certificate, prescribed in Civil Code Section 1189, should not be used for proofs of execution by subscribing witness.

Protests

Purpose. In rare instances, Notaries might be asked to protest a negotiable instrument for non-payment. A protest is a written statement by a Notary or other authorized officer verifying that payment was not received on an instrument such as a bank draft. Failure to pay is called dishonor. Before issuing a certificate of protest, the Notary must present the bank draft or other instrument to the person or entity obliged to pay, a procedure called presentment (Uniform Commercial Code, Section 3505).

Antiquated Act. In the 19th century, protests were common notarial acts in the United States, but they are rarely performed today due to the advent of modern electronic communications and resulting changes in our banking and financial systems. Modern Notaries most often encounter protests in the context of international commerce.

Prohibition. Effective January 1, 2012, only Notaries employed by a financial institution and performing a protest in the course of their employment may perform this notarial act.

Certificate for Protest. When a Notary protests a promissory note or bill of exchange for non-payment or non-acceptance, the protest certificate must include the following (Government Code, Section 8208):

1) The time and place of presentment of the bill or note.

2) That presentment was made and how presentment was made.

3) The cause or reason for protesting the bill or note.

4) The demand made and the answer given, if any, or the fact that the drawee or acceptor could not be found.

Protests from Out of State. When protesting bills of exchange or promissory notes, a California Notary may exercise any additional customary powers and duties prescribed by the other state or nation for that protest. This authorization applies only to protests and not to any other notarial act (Government Code, Section 8205).

PRACTICES AND PROCEDURES

Personal Appearance

Requirement. The principal signer must personally appear before the Notary at the time of the notarization. This means that the Notary and the signer must both be physically present, face to face in the same room, when the notarization takes place. Notarizations may never be performed over the telephone.

Willingness

Confirmation. The Notary should make every effort to confirm that the signer is acting willingly.

To confirm willingness, the Notary need only ask document signers if they are signing of their own free will. If a signer does or says anything that makes the Notary think the signer is being pressured to sign, the Notary should refuse to notarize.

Awareness

Confirmation. The Notary should make every effort to confirm that the signer is generally aware of what is taking place.

To confirm awareness, the Notary simply makes a layperson's judgment about the signer's ability to understand what is happening. A document signer who cannot respond intelligibly in a simple conversation with the Notary should not be considered sufficiently aware to sign at that moment. If the notarization is taking place in a medical environment, the signer's doctor can be consulted for a professional opinion. Otherwise, if the signer's awareness is in doubt, the Notary should refuse to notarize.

Identifying Document Signers

Satisfactory Evidence. In taking acknowledgments and executing jurats for any document, California law requires the Notary to identify the signer. The following two methods of identification constitute satisfactory evidence (Civil Code, Section 1185):

1) Reliable identification documents or ID cards. (See "Identification Documents," pages 27–28.)

2) The oath or affirmation of one *personally known* or two *unknown* credible identifying witnesses. (See "Credible Identifying Witness(es)," pages 28–30.)

In addition, satisfactory evidence means the absence of information or other circumstances that would lead a reasonable person to believe that the signer is not the individual he or she claims to be.

Verifying Representative Capacity. When performing an acknowledgment for a person signing in representation of another person or entity, a California Notary is not authorized to verify the capacity in which a person signs — such as corporate officer, trustee, partner to a partnership, attorney-in-fact or other representative capacity. The Notary only identifies the acknowledging signer as an individual.

Personal Knowledge of Identity

Not Acceptable. Notaries may not use personal knowledge to identify a signer for an acknowledgment or jurat or to identify a subscribing witness (Civil Code, Sections 1185 and 1196).

Identification Documents (ID Cards)

Acceptable Identification Documents. A Notary may identify a document signer for an acknowledgment or jurat with the following forms of written identification provided they are current or issued in the past five years (Civil Code, Section 1185):

- California driver's license or non-driver's ID issued by the California Department of Motor Vehicles

- U.S. passport book or card (physical description not required for either; signature not required for passport card)

- California Department of Corrections and Rehabilitation (CDCR) identification card for an inmate in custody in an institution in the state of California correctional system

- Effective January 1, 2016, any form of ID issued by a sheriff's department for a prisoner in custody in a county jail or local detention facility

A Notary may identify a document signer for an acknowledgment or jurat with the following forms of written identification provided they are current or issued in the past five years and contain a photograph, signature, serial or identifying number and physical description of the bearer (Civil Code, Section 1185):

- Foreign passport stamped by the U.S. Citizenship and Immigration Services (USCIS)

- Driver's license or non-driver's ID issued by another U.S. state

- Driver's license issued by Mexico or Canada

- Employee ID card issued by an agency or office of the State of California or any city, county or city and county within the state

- U.S. military ID that contains all required elements (The Common Access Card [CAC] — a replacement ID for certain military personnel — does not contain the signature of the bearer on either the front or back of the card.

Therefore, under current law, California Notaries may not accept the CAC as identification for notarizations.)

- ID cards issued by the USCIS (USCIS IDs may only be used to identify signers for notarizations on USCIS forms) (Government Code, Section 8230).

Unacceptable Identification Documents. Identification documents that are not acceptable for identifying signers include Social Security cards, credit cards, temporary driver's licenses and driver's licenses without photographs.

Name Variations. The Notary must make sure that the name on the document is the same as the name appearing on the identification presented. In certain circumstances, it may be acceptable for the name on the document to be an abbreviated form of the name on the ID — for example, John D. Smith instead of John David Smith. Last names or surnames, however, should always be the same.

Multiple Identification. While one good identification document may be sufficient to identify a signer, the Notary may ask for more.

Credible Identifying Witness(es)

Purpose. When a document signer is unable to present reliable ID cards, that signer may be identified on the oath (or affirmation) of one credible witness personally known to the Notary or two credible witnesses unknown to the Notary (Civil Code, Section 1185).

Qualifications. Every credible identifying witness must personally know the document signer.

A credible identifying witness must not have an interest, or be named, in the document. A credible identifying witness must know that the signer has no identification and that it would be impractical to obtain the necessary ID (Civil Code, Section 1185).

Credible Witness(es) Must Present ID. Every credible witness — known or unknown to the Notary — must present a valid state-approved ID card to the Notary.

A Notary who fails to require a personally known credible witness to present a valid state-approved ID is liable for a civil penalty of up to $10,000. This penalty may be brought by the Secretary of State in an administrative hearing or by a public prosecutor in superior court (Civil Code, Section 1185[b][1][B]).

Oath (Affirmation) for Credible Identifying Witness. To ensure truthfulness, the Notary must administer an oath or affirmation to each credible identifying witness. The credible identifying witness must swear or affirm that the following are true (Civil Code, Section 1185):

- The person making the acknowledgment or oath (affirmation) is the person named in the document.

- The person making the acknowledgment or oath (affirmation) is personally known to the witness.

- The person making the acknowledgment or oath (affirmation) does not possess any of the acceptable identification documents.

- The witness believes it is very difficult or impossible for the person making the acknowledgment or oath (affirmation) to obtain another form of identification.

- The witness does not have a financial interest in the document and is not named in the document.

An acceptable oath (affirmation) for a credible identifying witness might be:

> Do you solemnly swear that (signer) is the person named in the document; that (signer) is personally known to you; that it is your reasonable belief that the circumstances of (signer) are such that it would be very difficult or impossible for him/her to obtain another form of identification; that (signer) does not possess any of the acceptable identification documents; and that you do not have a financial interest nor are you named in the document, so help you God?
>
> (Do you solemnly affirm that [signer] is the person named in the document; that [signer] is personally known to you; that it is your reasonable belief that the circumstances of [signer] are such that it would be very difficult or impossible for him/her to obtain another form of identification; that [signer] does not possess any of the acceptable identification documents; and that you do not have a financial interest nor are you named in the document?)

Journal Entries for Credible Witnesses. If one credible witness is used to identify a signer, the credible witness must sign the Notary's journal or the Notary must record in the journal the type of identification presented by the witness, the government agency issuing the identification document, the document's serial or identifying number and the issuance or expiration date of the document (Government Code Section 8206[a][2][D]).

If two credible witnesses are used to identify a signer, the credible witness must sign the journal and the Notary Public must record each credible witness's identification information including the type of identification document used, the document's issuing agency, the serial or identifying number and the date of issuance or expiration (Government Code, Section 8206[a][2][E]).

While the law does not require a Notary to record the ID card information in the journal for one personally known credible witness who signs the journal, the National Notary Association recommends that the Notary include this information as well.

Not a Subscribing Witness. Notaries must not confuse credible identifying witnesses with subscribing witness. A credible identifying witness vouches for the identity of a signer who appears before the Notary. A subscribing witness vouches for the genuineness of the signature of a person who does not appear before the Notary. (See "Proof of Execution by Subscribing Witness," pages 22–24.)

Journal of Notarial Acts

Requirement. California Notaries are required to keep one active sequential journal of all of their official acts. A permanently bound record book (not loose-leaf) with numbered pages and entry spaces is best for preserving the sequence of notarial acts and for protecting against unauthorized removal of pages or tampering (Government Code, Section 8206).

Failure to Keep. Failure to keep a journal of notarial acts is reason for the Secretary of State to revoke, suspend or refuse to grant a Notary commission. In addition, a fine may be imposed. A Notary who willfully fails to properly maintain a journal of official acts is guilty of a misdemeanor (Government Code, Sections 8214.1, 8214.15 and 8228.1).

Journal Entries. Journal entries must be completed at the time of notarization, and a separate and complete entry must be recorded for each notarial act. Notaries may not use hash marks, ditto marks, arrows or other shortcuts to indicate information that is the same from one entry to the next, nor may they have someone for whom they notarized multiple documents sign the journal on a single diagonal line drawn across several entries.

Each journal entry must contain the following information (Government Code, Section 8206):

1) The date, time of day and type of notarization (jurat, acknowledgment, etc.).

2) The type of document notarized.

3) The signature of each person whose signature is notarized, including the signature of any subscribing witness.

4) A statement as to how the signer's identity was confirmed. The journal entry must contain either a description of the ID card accepted (including the type of ID, the government agency issuing the ID, the serial or identifying number and the date of issuance or expiration) or the required information for the credible identifying witness(es). (See "Credible Identifying Witness(es)," pages 28–30.)

5) The fee charged for the notarial service. Only the notarial fee should be entered in the fee column and it should never exceed the maximum amount, currently $10. If no fee is charged, the Notary must indicate this by recording "0," "no fee," "N/C" or the like.

6) For powers of attorney, deeds, quitclaim deeds, deeds of trust, and any document affecting any real property, the right thumbprint of each signer. (See "Documents Affecting Real Property," on pages 33–34 and 110–113, and "Journal Thumbprint Requirement," page 32.)

Document Dates. Although recording the document's date is not required by law, it is prudent to do so. So if the document has a specific date on it, the Notary should record that date in the journal of notarial acts.

Often the only date on a document is the date of the signature that is being notarized. If the signature is undated, however, the document may have no date on it at all. In that case, the Notary should record "no date" or "undated" in the journal.

For acknowledgments, the date the document was signed must either precede or be the same as the date of the notarization; it may not follow it. For a jurat, the date the document was signed and the date of the notarization must be the same.

A document whose signature is dated after the date on its Notary certificate risks rejection by a recorder, who may question how the document could have been notarized before it was signed.

Journal Signature. Perhaps the most important entry to obtain is the signer's signature. A journal signature protects the Notary against claims that a signer did not appear and is a deterrent to forgery, because it provides evidence of the signer's identity and appearance before the Notary.

To check for possible forgery, the Notary should compare the signature that the person leaves in the journal of notarial acts with the signatures on the document and on the IDs. The signatures should be at least reasonably similar.

The Notary also should observe the signing of the journal. If the signer appears to be laboring over the journal signature, this may be an indication of forgery in progress.

Journal Thumbprint Requirement. All signers of all powers of attorney as well as deeds, quitclaim deeds, deeds of trust and any document affecting any real property must leave a right thumbprint in the Notary's journal of notarial acts. A journal thumbprint is not required of signers of deeds of reconveyance and trustee's deeds resulting from a decree of foreclosure or a non-judicial foreclosure (Government Code, Section 8206).

If the signer's right thumbprint is not available, the Notary is required to obtain the left thumbprint or a print of any available finger. The Notary must note this in the journal. If the signer is physically unable to leave a thumbprint or a fingerprint, the Notary must note this in the journal with an explanation of the signer's physical condition (Government Code, Section 8206).

The journal thumbprint is a strong deterrent to forgery, because it represents absolute proof of the signer's identity. Provided the signer is willing, nothing prevents a Notary from asking for a thumbprint for every notarial act. However, it can only be made a precondition for notarizing when the document is a power of attorney, deed, quitclaim deed, deed of trust or other document affecting real property.

Documents Affecting Real Property. Because the language in California statute is quite broad, there are certain elements that may indicate a document is related to a real estate transaction and would require securing a journal thumbprint from the signer. These elements are:

- An Assessor's Parcel Number (APN) — An assessor's parcel number is a 10-digit number assigned to a parcel of real property by the tax assessor. This number could also be referred to as the assessor's identification number (AIN). A sample APN or AIN would be 2780-003-155. The APN is required by law on all deeds, trust deeds and mortgages.

- A legal property description — The written words which delineate a specific piece of real property, but not to be confused with a street address. A sample legal description is as follows:

  LOT 149 OF TRACT 9295, IN THE CITY OF LOS ANGELES AREA, COUNTY OF LOS ANGELES, STATE OF CALIFORNIA, AS PER MAP RECORDED IN BOOK 132, PAGE(S) 67 TO 69 INCLUSIVE OF SAID MAPS, IN THE OFFICE OF THE COUNTY RECORDER OF SAID COUNTY.

- A space in the margin for the recorder's use — Most real property documents that must be recorded in California must be acknowledged prior to recordation. To be submitted for recording in California, such documents must conform to certain recording requirements. All pages of the document must have at least half-inch margins on the two vertical sides. The first page of the document must have a top margin of at least 2½ inches. Of that 2½-inch space, the left half is used to show the name of the party requesting the recording and where to mail the document after it is recorded. The right half is reserved for the county recorder's stamp and indexing information. If a document is formatted in this fashion, it is a clue that the document affects real property.

- A cover sheet — On documents to be presented for recording that do not contain a top margin of 2½ inches of space that is reserved for the recorder's use, a separate cover sheet must be included. This cover sheet must show the name of the party requesting the recording, where to mail the document after it is recorded and the title or titles of the document.

In addition, certain estate planning documents such as wills and codicils, which are not typically notarized, or revocable or irrevocable trusts, which may be funded with the family home, would also be considered a document affecting real property. Please see the Documents List on pages 110–113 for a list of specific documents for which a journal thumbprint may be required.

Failure to Obtain Thumbprint. A Notary who willfully fails to obtain a thumbprint in the journal as required by law is subject to a civil penalty of up to $2,500. This fine may be brought either by the Secretary of State in an administrative hearing or by a public prosecutor in superior court (Government Code, Section 8214.23).

Complete Entry Before Certificate. The prudent Notary completes the journal entry before filling out the Notary certificate on a document. This prevents the signer from leaving with the notarized document before vital information can be entered in the journal.

Journal-Entry Copies. The law requires a Notary to provide a photocopy of a journal line item entry to any member of the public who presents a written request specifying the names of the parties, the type of document and the month and year the document was notarized (Government Code, Section 8206[c]).

Within 15 business days of receipt of a written request to provide a photocopy of an entry, a Notary must either provide the requested photocopy or acknowledge that no such line item exists (Government Code, Section 8206.5).

In a disciplinary proceeding for failure to provide either the line item or a response within 15 business days, a Notary may defend his or her delayed action on the basis of unavoidable, exigent business or personal circumstances (Government Code, Section 8206.5).

Copying by Employer. An employer of a Notary may request inspection or copies of journal entries that are directly related to the employer's business if the inspection or copying is done in the Notary's presence. An employer may ask a Notary-employee to regularly provide copies of business-related entries from the journal. The confidentiality and safekeeping of such journal copies are the employer's responsibility. The Notary cannot be required to allow inspection or provide copies of journal entries that are not related to the employer's business (Government Code, Section 8206[d]).

Answer Inquiries from State. Upon official written request, a Notary must send certified copies of journal entries to the Secretary of State within the time specified (Government Code, Section 8205[b][1]). (See "Certified Copies of Notarial Records," page 16.)

In addition, the Notary must respond within 30 days to any request from the Secretary of State sent by certified mail for information relating to official acts performed by the Notary (Government Code, Section 8205[b][2]).

Journal Security. The journal must be kept in a locked and secured area under the direct supervision and control of the Notary (Government Code, Section 8206).

Failure to secure the journal is reason for the Secretary of State to revoke, suspend or refuse to grant a Notary commission. In addition, a fine of up to $750 may be imposed (Government Code, Sections 8214.1 and 8214.15).

Lost or Stolen Journal. A Notary must immediately notify the Secretary of State by certified or registered mail if a journal is lost, stolen, misplaced, destroyed, damaged or otherwise rendered unusable. When notifying, the Notary must include his or her commission number and expiration date, the time period covered by the journal entries and a photocopy of any relevant police report (Government Code, Section 8206).

Surrendering Journal. Notaries should never surrender control of their official journals to anyone. Even when an employer has paid for the Notary's official journal — and regardless of whether the journal contains entries related to the employer's business — the journal stays with the Notary upon termination of employment. No person but the Notary may lawfully possess and use this official tool of the Notary's office (Government Code, Section 8206).

Law Enforcement Access. A peace officer who has reasonable suspicion or probable cause to believe the journal contains evidence of a crime or a criminal act may request the Notary to surrender or seize the journal. A Notary must surrender the journal to the peace officer immediately, or if the journal is not present as soon as possible thereafter. Any requirements of, or exceptions to, state and federal law will apply to an officer who seizes a journal (Government Code, Sections 8206[d] and [f]).

A peace officer is defined by Penal Code Sections 830.1, 830.2 and 830.3.

A Notary may be fined up to $2,500 for willfully failing to provide access to the journal when requested by a peace officer. This fine may be imposed by the Secretary of State in an administrative proceeding or a public prosecutor in superior court (Government Code, Section 8214.21).

<u>If Journal Is Seized</u>. If the Notary's journal is seized by a peace officer, the Notary must obtain a receipt for the relinquished journal from the peace officer and notify the Secretary of State by certified mail within 10 days. The notification must include the period of the journal entries, the Notary's commission number and expiration date, and a photocopy of the receipt.

Upon surrendering the journal to a peace officer, the Notary must obtain a new journal, and if the seized journal is returned, the Notary may not use it to record any new entries (Government Code, Section 8206[d]).

<u>Disposition of Notarial Records</u>. If a Notary resigns, is disqualified, is removed from office or allows the Notary's commission to expire without obtaining another commission within 30 days, then his or her notarial records must be delivered to the county clerk's office where the Notary's oath of office and bond are on file within 30 days of commission resignation, revocation or expiration.

The Los Angeles County Board of Supervisors recently adopted an ordinance directing the County Registrar-Recorder/Clerk to charge $10 for surrendering Notary journals (Los Angeles County Ordinance 2011-025). The fee is for all journals surrendered at one time. California statute authorizes other California counties to charge for surrendering journals, but at the time of this printing, the National Notary Association is unaware of any other county with a journal disposition fee.

If a Notary refuses to deliver notarial records to the county clerk as specified by law, the Notary is guilty of a misdemeanor and is liable for damages suffered by any person as a result.

If the Notary dies, the Notary's executor or personal representative must promptly notify the Secretary of State and deliver all the decedent's notarial records and papers to the county clerk's office where the Notary's oath and bond are filed.

After 10 years, the office of the county clerk may destroy the notarial records upon court order. Notaries may never destroy their notarial records (Government Code, Section 8209).

Destruction of Notarial Records. It is a misdemeanor for any person to purposely destroy, deface or conceal a Notary's journal. A person who does so is liable for damages suffered by any person as a result (Government Code, Sections 8209 and 8221).

Notary Certificate

Requirement. In notarizing any document, a Notary must complete a Notary certificate. The certificate is wording that indicates exactly what the Notary has certified. The Notary certificate may either be printed on the document itself or on an attachment. The certificate should contain:

1) A *venue* indicating where the notarization is performed. "State of California, County of _____," is the typical venue wording, with the county name inserted in the blank. The letters "SS." or "SCT." sometimes appear after the venue; they abbreviate the traditional Latin word *scilicet,* meaning "in particular" or "namely."

2) A *statement of particulars* indicating what the notarization has attested to. An acknowledgment certificate would include such wording as:

"On _____ before me, (here insert name and title of the officer), personally appeared _____, who proved to me on the basis of satisfactory evidence to be the person(s) whose name(s) is/are subscribed to the within instrument and acknowledged to me...."

A jurat certificate would include such wording as:

"Subscribed and sworn to (or affirmed) before me on this _____ day of _____ (month), _____ (year), by _____, proved to me on the basis of satisfactory evidence to be the person(s)...."

3) A *testimonium clause*, which may be optional if the date is included in the statement of particulars: "Witness my hand and official seal, this _____ day of _____ (month), ____ (year)." In this short sentence, the Notary formally

attests to the truthfulness of the preceding facts in the certificate. "Hand" means signature.

4) The *official signature* of the Notary, exactly as the name appears on the Notary's commission.

5) The *official seal* of the Notary, placed near but not over the Notary's signature.

Completing the Certificate. When filling in the blanks in the Notary certificate, Notaries should either type or print neatly in dark ink.

Notaries also must pay attention to places on the Notary certificate that indicate the number and gender of the document signers, as well as how they were identified — for example, leave the plural "(s)" untouched or cross it out, as appropriate.

Correcting a Certificate. When filling out the certificate, the Notary needs to make sure any preprinted information is accurate. For example, the venue — the state and county in which the notarial act is taking place — may have been filled in prior to the notarization. If the preprinted venue is incorrect, the Notary must line through the incorrect state and/or county, write in the proper site of the notarization, and initial and date the change.

Certificate Forms. When certificate wording is not preprinted on the document, or when preprinted wording is not acceptable, the Notary may attach a certificate form. This form typically is stapled to the document's left margin following the signature page.

If the certificate form is replacing unacceptable preprinted wording, the Notary should line through the preprinted wording and write below it, "See attached certificate." If the document has no preprinted wording, however, the Notary should not add this notation. Those words could be viewed as an unauthorized change to the document.

To prevent a certificate form from being removed and fraudulently placed on another document, the Notary may add a brief description of the document to the certificate: "This certificate is attached to a _____ (title or type of document), dated _____ (date), of _____ (number) pages, signed by _____ (name[s] of signer[s])."

The National Notary Association offers certificate forms that have similar wording preprinted on them; otherwise, the Notary will have to print, type, or stamp this information on each certificate form used. Finally, when Notaries attach a certificate form to a document, they should always note in their journals that they did so, as well as the means by which they attached the certificate to the document: "Certificate form stapled to document, following signature page."

While fraud-deterrent steps such as these can make it much more difficult for a certificate form to be removed and misused, there is no absolute protection against its removal and misuse. While a certificate form remains in their control, however, Notaries must absolutely ensure that it is attached only to its intended document.

Selecting Certificates. Non-attorney Notaries should never select Notary certificates for any transaction. It is not the role of a non-attorney Notary to decide what type of certificate — and thus what type of notarization — a document needs. As ministerial officials, Notaries generally follow instructions and complete forms that have been provided for them; they do not issue instructions or decide which forms are appropriate in a given case.

If a document is presented to a Notary without certificate wording and if the signer does not know what type of notarial act is appropriate, the signer should be asked to find out what kind of notarization and certificate are needed. Usually the agency that issued or will be accepting the document can provide this information. A Notary who selects certificates may be engaging in the unauthorized practice of law.

Do Not Pre-Sign or Pre-Seal Certificates. A Notary must never sign and/or seal certificates ahead of time or permit other persons to attach Notary certificate forms to documents.

A Notary must never give or mail an unattached, signed, and sealed certificate form to another person and trust that person to attach it to a particular document, even if asked to do so by a signer who previously appeared before the Notary.

These actions could facilitate fraud or forgery, and, since such actions would be indefensible in a civil court of law, they could subject the Notary to lawsuits to recover damages resulting from the Notary's neglect or misconduct. In addition, the Secretary of State could fine the Notary up to $750 and revoke, suspend or refuse to renew the Notary's commission (Government Code, Section 8214.1 and Civil Code, Section 1188).

Standard Size for Certificates. Additional recording fees will be charged for documents when any page of the document, including the attached Notary certificate, is not the standard 8½ by 11-inch size. The extra fee is $3 per page and is applied to all pages of the document. The person who files the document, not the Notary, is responsible for the extra fees (Government Code, Sections 27361 and 27361.5).

False Certificate or Writing. A Notary who knowingly completes a certificate or executes a writing containing statements the Notary knows are false may be charged with a misdemeanor. A misdemeanor charge may be brought within four years after discovery of the violation, or within four years after completion of the offense, whichever is later (Government Code, Section 6203).

In addition, any Notary who knowingly completes a false acknowledgment certificate may be charged with forgery (Penal Code, Section 470).

Furthermore, a Notary may have his or her commission revoked for executing a certificate containing information the Notary knows is false and may be fined up to $1,500 (Government Code, Section 8214.1)

Finally, a Notary who willfully states as true any material fact that he or she knows is false may be fined up to $10,000. This penalty may be imposed by the Secretary of State in an administrative hearing or by a public prosecutor in superior court (Civil Code, Section 1189).

Notary Seal

Requirement. A California Notary must affix an impression of an official seal on the certificate portion of every document notarized (Government Code, Section 8207).

Format. The seal may be either circular and not more than two inches in diameter or rectangular and not more than an inch in height and 2½ inches in length. In either case, it must have a serrated or milled edged border (Government Code, Section 8207).

Inking and Embossing Seals. The seal must imprint or emboss a photographically reproducible impression. Because the image must be photocopiable, most Notaries use an inked rubber-stamp seal, since an embossment would have to be smudged or darkened to be picked up on camera. An embossing seal may be used in addition to the required photographically reproducible seal, but it must not be used over the reproducible inking seal or over the Notary's signature (Government Code, Section 8207).

Required Information. The seal impression must clearly show the following information (Government Code, Section 8207):

- Name of the Notary (exactly as it appears on the commission certificate).

- The circular California state seal.

- The words "Notary Public."

- The county where the Notary's oath and bond are filed.

- The Notary's commission expiration date.

- The Notary's commission number.

- The ID number of the seal manufacturer or vendor.

Placement of Seal Impression. The Notary's official seal impression should be placed near but not over the Notary's signature on the Notary certificate. It must be easily readable and should not be placed over signatures or any printed matter on the document. An illegible or improperly placed seal may result in rejection of the document by a recorder. (See "Recording Requirements," page 42.)

If there is no room for the seal, the Notary may have no choice but to complete and attach a certificate form that duplicates the notarial wording on the document.

L.S. On many certificates the letters "L.S." appear, indicating where the seal is to be placed. These letters abbreviate the Latin term *locus sigilli*, meaning "place of the seal." An inking seal or photographically reproducible embossing seal should be placed near but not over the letters, so that wording imprinted by the seal will not be obscured. A non-photographically reproducible embossing seal, used in conjunction with an inking seal, may be placed directly over the letters, slightly displacing portions of the characters and leaving a clue that document examiners can use to distinguish an original from a forged photocopy.

Illegible Seal. If an initial seal impression is unreadable and there is ample room on the document, another impression can be affixed nearby. The illegibility of the first impression will indicate why a second seal impression was necessary. The Notary should then record in the journal that a second impression was applied.

A Notary should never attempt to fix an imperfect seal impression with pen, ink or correction fluid. This may be viewed as evidence of tampering and cause the document to be rejected by a receiving agency.

Recording Requirements. If a Notary fails to use a photographically reproducible seal, the document may be accepted for recording in a California county if an embossing seal is present and legible and if the Notary has printed or typed the following below or adjacent to the Notary's signature: the Notary's name, the county of the Notary's principal place of business, the Notary's telephone number, the Notary's commission number and the Notary's commission expiration date (Government Code, Section 66436).

Plastic Subdivision Maps. Because many seal inks smear on plastic-surfaced subdivision maps, acknowledgment certificates printed on such maps need not bear the Notary's seal if the Notary's name, county of principal place of business and commission expiration date are typed or printed below or immediately adjacent to the Notary's signature (Government Code, Section 66436).

Certificate of Authorization. No person may purchase a California Notary seal without first presenting to the approved seal vendor a "Certificate of Authorization to Manufacture Notary Public Seals," issued by the Secretary of State. This certificate is sent to each newly commissioned Notary, along with the commissioning papers (Government Code, Section 8207.2).

The seal vendor must keep a copy of each Certificate of Authorization presented and a record of each Notary's ID number. The vendor must submit the original Certificate of Authorization, containing a sample impression of the new seal, to the Secretary of State for verification of the vendor's authority to manufacture a seal and for recordkeeping (Government Code, Section 8207.3).

The failure of a Notary or vendor to comply with the procedures regarding the Certificate of Authorization can result in a $1,500 fine for each violation. Such a penalty would result from a civil lawsuit initiated by the Attorney General or a local district attorney, city attorney or prosecutor (Government Code, Section 8207.4).

Lost or Damaged Seal. Any Notary whose official seal is lost, misplaced, destroyed, broken, damaged or otherwise unworkable must immediately mail or deliver written notice to the Secretary of State, who will issue a Certificate of Authorization to obtain a replacement. Failure to report can result in a $1,500 fine (Government Code, Section 8207.4).

Seal Security. The seal must be kept in a locked and secured area under the direct supervision and control of the Notary. Failure to secure the seal is reason for the Secretary of State to revoke, suspend or refuse to grant a Notary commission. In addition, a fine of up to $750 may be imposed. A Notary who willfully fails to safeguard the seal, or who surrenders the seal to any person not authorized to possess it, is guilty of a misdemeanor. A misdemeanor charge may be brought within four years after discovery of the violation, or within four years after completion of the offense, whichever is later (Government Code, Sections 8207, 8214.1, 8214.15 and 8228.1).

Misuse of Seal. Any person who, with intent to defraud, forges or counterfeits a Notary seal to give a document the appearance of being government-issued is guilty of forgery. Documents may include, but are not limited to, an identification card, driver's license, birth certificate, passport or Social Security card. Forgery is punishable by imprisonment for up to one year (Penal Code, Sections 470, 472 and 473).

Use of Seal for Endorsement or Testimonial. Notaries may not use the official seal to endorse or promote any product, service or contest. The Notary seal may only be used to carry out the official duties of a Notary Public (Government Code, Section 8207).

Electronic Seal. Documents that now can be notarized and transmitted electronically to the recorder by a "trusted submitter" include substitutions of trustee, assignments of a deed of trust and reconveyance deeds — but no others. A trusted submitter is a title insurer; underwritten title company; institutional lender; or local, state or federal governmental entity. Notaries are permitted to notarize these electronic documents without affixing a physical Notary seal image to the form as long as the information contained in the Notary seal is included with the Notary's electronic signature (Government Code, Section 578). (See "Electronic Signatures," pages 59–60.)

Fees for Notarial Services

Maximum Fees. The following maximum fees are authorized for California Notaries:

- Acknowledgments — $10. For taking an acknowledgment, the maximum fee is $10 for each signature notarized. For notarizing a single document with signatures of three persons appearing before the Notary, a maximum of $30 could be charged (Government Code, Section 8211).

- Certified Copy of Power of Attorney — $10. A maximum of $10 per copy may be charged by a Notary for certifying a copy of a power of attorney (Government Code, Section 8211).

- Copy of Journal Entry — 30¢. A maximum of 30 cents per photocopy may be charged for providing a photocopy of an entry in the Notary's journal (Government Code, Section 8206).

- Depositions — $20. For all services rendered in taking a deposition, the maximum fee is $20, plus $5 for administering an oath to the witness and $5 for completing the certificate on the deposition (Government Code, Section 8211).

- Immigration Papers — $10 per set. A non-attorney Notary bonded as an immigration consultant may not charge more than $10 per set of forms (apart from the standard notarial fee) for entering data provided by a client on state or federal immigration forms. Violators may be fined up to $750 (Government Code, Sections 8214.1, 8214.15 and 8223).

- <u>Jurats</u> — $10. For executing a jurat, including the administration of the oath or affirmation, the fee is not to exceed $10 per signature notarized (Government Code, Section 8211).

- <u>Oaths and Affirmations</u> — $10. For administering an oath or affirmation, with or without completion of a jurat, the maximum fee is $10 per oath (Government Code, Section 8211).

- <u>Proofs of Execution by Subscribing Witness</u> — $10. For taking a proof of execution, including the administration of the oath or affirmation, the maximum fee is the same as for an acknowledgment: $10 for each signature of the principal proven by a subscribing witness (Government Code, Section 8211).

<u>Option Not to Charge</u>. Notaries are not required to charge for their notarial services, and they may charge any fee less than the maximum. However, Notaries employed by some public agencies may be required by their employers to charge for their services and to remit the fees to the employer (Government Code, Section 6100).

<u>Overcharging</u>. Charging more than the legally prescribed fees is reason for the Secretary of State to revoke, suspend or refuse to grant a Notary commission. In addition, a fine of up to $750 may be imposed (Government Code, Sections 8214.1 and 8214.15).

<u>Travel Fees</u>. Charges for travel by a Notary are not specified by law. Such fees are allowed only if the Notary and signer agree beforehand on the amount to be charged. The Notary should tell the signer that a travel fee is not stated in the law and is separate from the notarial fees.

<u>Obligation to Itemize</u>. A Notary employed by a county or judicial district is required to make out a receipt for notarial fees for any person requesting one. The Notary is liable for three times the notarial fee for neglecting or refusing to honor such a request (Government Code, Section 6109).

Failure to Complete Notarization. For failing or refusing to complete a lawful request for notarization once payment is offered for it, a Notary is liable for any resulting ramifications (Government Code, Section 6110).

Fee Not Allowed. No fee may be charged for notarizing absentee ballots or other voting materials (Government Code, Section 8211), or a nomination document or circulator's affidavit (Election Code, Section 8080).

A U.S. military veteran may not be charged for notarization of a claim for any veteran's benefit (Government Code, Section 8211).

Blank or Incomplete Documents

Do Not Notarize. California Notaries are prohibited from taking an acknowledgment or a proof of execution of any document that is not complete (Government Code, Section 8205).

Any blanks in a document should be filled in by the signer prior to notarization. If the blanks are inapplicable and intended to be left unfilled, the signer should line through each space or write "Not Applicable" or "N/A." The Notary may not, however, tell the signer what to write in the blanks. If the signer is unsure how to fill in the blanks, he or she should contact the document's issuer, its eventual recipient, or an attorney.

Photocopies & Faxes

Original Signature. A photocopy or fax may be notarized as long as the signature on it is original, meaning that the photocopy or fax must have been signed with pen and ink. Signatures on documents presented for notarization must always be signed with a handwritten, original signature. A photocopied or faxed signature may never be notarized.

Public recorders sometimes will not accept notarized photocopies or faxes, because the text of the document may be too faint to adequately reproduce in microfilming.

Disqualifying Interest

Financial or Beneficial Interest. A Notary may not perform any notarization related to a transaction in which that Notary has a direct financial or beneficial interest (Government Code, Section 8224).

A financial or beneficial interest exists when the Notary is named in a financial transaction or when the Notary receives, as a result of the transaction, an advantage, right, privilege, property or fee valued in excess of the lawfully prescribed notarial fee.

In regard to real estate transactions, a Notary is considered to have a disqualifying financial or beneficial interest when that Notary is a grantor or grantee, a mortgagor or mortgagee, a trustor or trustee, a vendor or vendee, a lessor or lessee or a beneficiary of the transaction.

Exemptions. Certain persons are exempt from this beneficial and financial interest provision. A Notary who is an agent, employee, insurer, attorney, escrow officer or lender for a person signing a document may notarize the document without being considered to have a disqualifying interest. For example, a real estate agent can notarize a document relating to a property transfer even if the agent derives a commission from that transaction.

Any challenged case of disqualifying financial or beneficial interest would be decided in court. Thus, it is always safest for a Notary to ensure that he or she has no financial or beneficial interest whatsoever in a transaction regardless of what the law allows (Government Code, Section 8224).

Relatives. Although California state law does not expressly prohibit notarizing for a relative, the National Notary Association strongly advises against doing so for persons related by blood or marriage. Family matters often involve a financial or other beneficial interest that may not be readily apparent at the time of notarization.

Notarizing for family members may also challenge the Notary's ability to act impartially. For example, a Notary who is asked to notarize a contract signed by his or her brother might attempt to persuade him to sign or not sign. A sibling is entitled to exert influence, but this is entirely improper for a Notary.

Even if a Notary has no interest in the document and does not attempt to influence the signer, notarizing for a relative could subject the document to a legal challenge if other parties to the transaction allege the Notary could not have acted impartially.

Refusal of Services

Lawful Requests. Upon payment of the fees required by law, Notaries must honor all lawful and reasonable requests to notarize. A Notary may be liable for every refusal to do so (Government Code, Section 6110).

Discrimination. A person's race, age, gender, religion, nationality, ethnicity, lifestyle or political viewpoint is never legitimate cause for refusing to perform a notarial act. A Notary may be liable for every refusal to do so.

Exception for Employer/Notary Agreement. A Notary and employer may agree to limit the Notary's services solely to transactions directly related to the employer's business during business hours (Government Code, Section 8202.8). Notary-employees may refuse to notarize for non-customers if they have entered into this type of agreement with their employer. (See "Employer/Notary Agreement," below.)

Reasonable Care

Responsibility. As public servants, Notaries must act responsibly and exercise reasonable care in the performance of their official duties. If a Notary fails to do so, he or she may be subject to a civil lawsuit to recover financial damages caused by his or her error or omission.

In general, reasonable care is a degree of concern and attentiveness that a person of normal intelligence and responsibility would exhibit. If a Notary can show a judge or jury that he or she did everything expected of a reasonable person, the judge or jury is obligated by law to find the Notary not liable for damages.

Complying with all pertinent laws is the first rule of reasonable care for a Notary. If there are no statutory guidelines in a given instance, the Notary should use common sense and prudence.

Employer/Notary Agreement

Agreement to Limit Notary's Services. A private employer who has paid for an employee-Notary's commission, bond, seal and other supplies may limit the Notary's services during business hours solely to transactions directly related to the employer's business, if the Notary agrees (Government Code, Sections 8202.7 and 8202.8).

It may be helpful to the Notary to have this agreement in writing to prevent requests for exceptions when limiting services.

Fees. A Notary who enters into such an agreement with a private employer may agree to hand over the notarial fees to the employer. The law requires the employer to place those fees into the account from which the Notary is paid (Government Code, Section 8202.7).

Not Applicable to Government Employees. Employer/Notary agreements do not apply to government-employee Notaries.

Notarizing a Signature by Mark

Mark Serves as Signature. A person who is unable to sign his or her name may instead use a mark — an "X" for example — as a signature, as long as there are two witnesses to the making of the mark (Civil Code, Section 14).

Witnesses. For a mark to be notarized, two witnesses to the making of the mark are required. Both witnesses must sign the document, and one witness must print legibly the marker's name beside the mark on the document (Civil Code, Section 14).

Journal Entry. The marker must make his or her mark in the Notary's journal. This mark must be witnessed by one person, and the witness must print the marker's name next to the mark and then sign the journal as a witness (Civil Code Section 14).

Although not a requirement of law, the National Notary Association recommends that the Notary record the names of the witnesses to a signature by mark in the journal entry for the transaction and have both witnesses sign the journal.

Witnesses' Statement. For a document to be filed in California, county recorders require the witnesses to sign a statement on the document confirming the particulars of the procedure. This statement is in addition to the Notary certificate. California county recorders prefer the following wording:

_____ (name of signer), being unable to write, made his/her mark in our presence and requested the first of the undersigned to write his/her name, which he/she did, and we now subscribe our names as witnesses thereto.

_____ (Signature of witness #1)
_____ (Signature of witness #2)

Signature-by-Mark Certificate. A properly witnessed mark is considered a valid signature under law, so no special Notary certificate is required. For acknowledgments filed in California, Notaries must use the California Acknowledgment form; jurats require the prescribed jurat wording.

Notarizing for Minors

Under Age 18. Generally, persons must reach the age of majority before they can handle their own legal affairs and sign documents for themselves. In California, the age of majority is 18. Normally, parents or guardians will sign on a minor's behalf. In certain cases, where minors are engaged in business transactions or serving as court witnesses, they may lawfully sign documents and have their signatures notarized.

Include Age Next to Signature. When notarizing for a minor, the Notary should ask the young signer to write his or her age next to the signature to alert any person relying upon the document that the signer is a minor. The Notary is not required to verify the minor signer's age.

Identification. The method for identifying a minor is the same as that for an adult. Because minors often do not possess acceptable identification documents, such as driver's licenses or passports, determining the identity of a minor can be a problem. If the minor does not have an acceptable ID, then another form of satisfactory evidence must be used (e.g., one personally known or two unknown credible identifying witnesses). (See "Credible Identifying Witness(es)," pages 28–30.)

Authentication

Documents Sent Out of State. Documents notarized in California and sent to other states may be required to bear proof that the Notary's signature and seal are genuine and that the Notary had authority to act at the time of notarization. This process of proving the genuineness of an official signature and seal is called authentication or legalization.

In California, proof of the Notary's commission is in the form of an authenticating certificate attached to a notarized document by either the county clerk's office where the Notary's oath and bond are filed or the Secretary of State's office. These certificates are also known as certificates of authority, certificates of capacity, certificates of authenticity, certificates of prothonotary and "flags."

The fee for an authenticating certificate from the county clerk will vary from county to county. An authenticating certificate from the Secretary of State costs $20 through the mail (check made out to "Secretary of State") and takes about two weeks to process. The original notarized document, a cover letter indicating the destination of the document, and an addressed, postage-paid return envelope must be included. This should all be sent to:

>Office of Secretary of State
>Notary Public Section
>P.O. Box 942877
>Sacramento, CA 94277-0001

In person, an authenticating certificate from the California Secretary of State may be obtained at 1500 11th Street, 2nd Floor, in Sacramento. For in-person pickup and processing while you wait, the cost is $26. An appointment is not necessary. It is not the Notary's responsibility to pick up or pay for the certificate of authority. Additional information is available on the Secretary of State's website in the Notary Public Section at *www.sos.ca.gov/notary/authentication*.

Documents Sent Out of Country. If the notarized document is going outside the United States, a chain authentication process may be necessary, and additional certificates of authority may have to be obtained from the U.S. Department of State in Washington, D.C., a foreign consulate in Washington, D.C. and a ministry of foreign affairs in the particular foreign nation.

Apostilles and the Hague Convention. More than 100 nations, including the United States, subscribe to a treaty under the auspices of the Hague Conference that simplifies authentication of notarized documents exchanged between these nations. The official name of this treaty, adopted by the Conference on October 5, 1961, is *The Hague Convention Abolishing the Requirement of Legalization for Foreign Public Documents*. (For a list of the subscribing countries, visit *www.hcch.net/index_en.php*.)

Under the Hague Convention, only one authenticating certificate called an *apostille* is necessary to ensure acceptance in these subscribing countries. (*Apostille* is French for "notation.")

In California, *apostilles* are issued by the Secretary of State's office. The procedure and fees are the same as for obtaining an ordinary authenticating certificate. Ensure that the country for which the document is destined is also specified.

Unauthorized Practice of Law

Do Not Assist in Legal Matters. A Notary who is not an attorney may not give legal advice or accept fees for legal advice. The non-attorney Notary may not assist a signer to draft, prepare, select, complete or understand a document or transaction. A Notary may only be responsible for the information on the Notary certificate.

Notaries may complete legal documents in which they are named as a subscribing party, but may never notarize their own signatures. Notaries involved in the unauthorized practice of law may have their commissions revoked and be criminally prosecuted (Government Code, Section 8214.1 and Business and Professions Code, Section 6125).

Exceptions. Non-attorney Notaries who are specially trained, certified or licensed in a particular field (e.g., real estate) may offer advice in that field only. Paralegals under the supervision of an attorney may give advice about documents in routine legal matters.

Advertising

False or Misleading Advertising. A Notary's commission can be revoked or suspended if the Notary uses false or misleading advertising to misrepresent the authority, rights and privileges of a Notary. In addition, a fine of up to $1,500 may be imposed (Government Code, Sections 8214.1 and 8214.15).

Foreign-Language Advertising. A non-attorney Notary advertising notarial services in a foreign language must take steps to guard against misinterpretation of his or her function as a Notary. Non-attorney Notaries are required to include in any such foreign-language advertisement the following, in both English and the foreign language (Government Code, Section 8219.5):

1) The statement: "I am not an attorney and, therefore, cannot give legal advice about immigration or any other legal matters."

2) The fees that a Notary is allowed to charge.

These requirements apply to signs and all other forms of written communication (business cards, telephone book ads) with the exception of a single desk plaque. Furthermore, literal translation of "Notary Public" into Spanish (*Notario Publico*) is prohibited by law. On the first violation, a Notary's commission must be suspended for a year or revoked and the Notary may incur a $1,500 penalty. On the second offense, the Notary's commission must be revoked permanently (Government Code, Section 8219.5 and Business and Professions Code, Sections 22442.3).

In addition, a non-attorney Notary who literally translates "Notary Public" into Spanish will be subject to a civil penalty not to exceed $1,000 per day for each violation to be assessed and collected in a civil action brought by the California State Bar (Business and Professions Code, Section 6126.7).

Immigration Expert. No person who claims to be an immigration expert or counselor may also advertise as a Notary Public. This provision attempts to prevent immigration counselors from misrepresenting their authority. Violators may be fined up to $1,500 (Government Code, Section 8223).

Foreign Languages

Foreign-Language Documents. California Notaries are not expressly prohibited from notarizing a non-English document. There are, however, difficulties to consider with foreign-language documents: A blatant fraud might be undetectable, the U.S. Notary seal might be misinterpreted in another country, and making a complete journal entry might be difficult.

Ideally, a foreign-language document should be referred to a Notary who reads that language. In many states, the website of the Notary-regulating official has a Notary directory. These directories often include the foreign languages read or spoken by each Notary listed.

California Notaries are required to use Notary certificates worded exactly as they appear in statute for acknowledgments on documents filed in California and for jurats and proofs of execution on any document, regardless of where it will be filed (Government Code, Section 8202, and Civil Code, Sections 1189 and 1195). Therefore, Notary certificates for these notarial acts must be in English. According to the California Secretary of

State, Notary certificates for acknowledgments on documents filed out of state also must be in English: Foreign-language acknowledgment certificates are not acceptable.

   Foreign-Language Signers. There must always be direct communication between the Notary and document signer, whether in English or another language. The Notary should never rely upon an intermediary or interpreter to determine a signer's willingness or awareness. A third party may have reasons to misrepresent the transaction to the Notary and/or to the signer.

Immigration

   Documents. Certain immigration documents may be notarized. However, state law places certain restrictions on the Notary in the area of immigration. Notaries must strictly adhere to these laws.
   A non-attorney Notary who is also bonded as an immigration consultant may enter data provided by a client on state or federal immigration forms. Notaries who enter data in immigration forms without also being bonded as an immigration consultant may be fined up to $1,500 (Government Code, Sections 8214.1, 8214.15(a) and 8223).

   Advertising. No person who claims to be an immigration expert or counselor may also advertise as a Notary Public. This provision is designed to prevent immigration counselors from misrepresenting their powers to unsuspecting foreigners. Violators may have their Notary commissions revoked or suspended or be fined up to $1,500 (Government Code, Sections 8214.1, 8214.15 and 8223 and Business and Professions Code, Section 22442.3).

   Identifying Signers. In notarizing forms that will be submitted to the U.S. Citizenship and Immigration Services (USCIS), a Notary may accept as proof of identity any ID or documentation acceptable to the USCIS (Government Code, Section 8230).

   Naturalization Certificates. It is unlawful for a Notary to make copies of naturalization certificates. Certified true copy of a certificate of naturalization must be requested at the local USCIS.

   False Statement on Immigration Document. It is a misdemeanor for any person (including a Notary) to knowingly, and for payment, make a false statement on a document related to immigration.

The person may be imprisoned in a county jail for a maximum of six months, be fined up to $2,500, or both (Penal Code, Section 653.55).

Military-Base Notaries

Qualifications. The Secretary of State may appoint Notaries for military bases of the U.S. Army, Navy, Coast Guard, Air Force and Marine Corps in the state. These military-base Notaries must (Government Code, Sections 8203.1 to 8203.3):

1) Be citizens of the United States.

2) Be at least 18 years old.

3) Have successfully completed the Notary examination.

4) Be federal civil service employees at the base where they will act.

5) Receive the recommendation of the base commanding officer.

6) Have completed a state-approved education course on the Notary's duties and functions.

Term of Office. The military-base Notary is commissioned for four years. However, this person ceases to be a Notary whenever he or she ceases to be employed as a civil service employee at the base where appointed. The commanding officer must notify the Secretary of State within 30 days of termination of the Notary's employment (Government Code, Section 8203.4).

Jurisdiction. Military-base Notaries can notarize only at the base where they were appointed (Government Code, Section 8203.2).

Fees. Military-base Notaries may not charge for notarial services (Government Code, Section 8203.6).

Certificates. On Notary certificates, military-base Notaries must include the name of the base where the document was notarized (Government Code, Section 8203.5).

Wills

<u>Do Not Offer Advice</u>. Often, people attempt to draw up wills without benefit of legal counsel and then bring these homemade testaments to a Notary to have them "legalized," expecting the Notary to know how to proceed. In advising or assisting such persons, the Notary risks prosecution for the unauthorized practice of law and the Notary's ill-informed advice may do considerable damage to the affairs of the signer.

Wills are highly sensitive documents, the format of which is dictated by strict laws. The slightest deviation from these laws can nullify a will. In some cases, holographic (handwritten) wills have actually been voided by notarization.

<u>Do Not Proceed Without Certificate Wording</u>. A Notary may notarize a will if the would-be testator is following the advice of an attorney, but only if notarial wording is provided. The Notary cannot advise the signer on how to proceed. Wills probated in California generally do not require notarization, though they must be witnessed. However, a California Notary may be asked to notarize a will that will be probated in another state.

<u>Living Wills</u>. Documents popularly called living wills may be notarized upon request. These are not actual wills; they are a form of advance health care directive, in which the signer gives instructions for medical treatment in the event that he or she becomes unable to personally provide such instructions due to illness or incapacity.

Durable Power of Attorney for Health Care

<u>Health Care Proxy</u>. A durable power of attorney for health care is another form of advance health care directive. This type of directive differs from a living will in that it appoints a specific person to make decisions on behalf of a principal (the signer) in the event that the principal becomes unable to do so due to illness or incapacity.

<u>Signing Requirements</u>. To be legally valid, a durable power of attorney for health care must contain the date of signing and must be signed either by the principal or (if the principal cannot sign) in the principal's name by another adult in the principal's presence and under his or her direction. The power of attorney must be either acknowledged before a Notary or signed by two witnesses.

Notarization. If the principal chooses to acknowledge the power of attorney before a Notary, then the principal must leave his or her right thumbprint in the Notary's journal.

Witness Requirements. If witnesses are used, they must be adults, must witness the signing or acknowledgment of the instrument and must sign a witness's statement as prescribed by Probate Code Section 4701.

At least one witness must be a person who is not related to the principal by blood, marriage or adoption and does not have an interest in the principal's estate.

In addition, the following persons may not act as a witness (Probate Code, Sections 4122 and 4701):

- The principal's attorney-in-fact

- The principal's health care provider or an employee of that health care provider

- The operator or an employee of a community or residential care facility

Skilled Nursing Facility. If a durable power of attorney is executed by a patient in a skilled nursing facility, a patient advocate or ombudsman must sign either as one of the two required witnesses, or in addition to the notarization. The patient advocate or ombudsman must declare that he or she is serving as a witness in accordance with the provisions of Probate Code, Section 4675 (Probate Code, Section 4701).

A "skilled nursing facility" is defined in the California Health and Safety Code, Section 1250(a)(2)(c), as "a health facility that provides skilled nursing care and supportive care to patients whose primary need is for availability of skilled nursing care on an extended basis."

Electronic Power of Attorney for Health Care. An electronic durable power of attorney for health care is legally valid if it meets the same requirements as a written power of attorney. However, the electronic instrument must be acknowledged by the principal before a Notary Public; two witnesses may not be used instead (Probate Code, Section 4673).

The electronic durable power of attorney for health care would be signed with an electronic signature by both the principal and the Notary. (See "Electronic Signatures," pages 59–60.) While any type of electronic signature technology may be used, Probate Code Section 4673 prescribes certain rules for digital signatures. (See "Digital Signatures," page 59.)

If a digital signature is used in executing the power of attorney, it must:

- Meet the requirements of Government Code Section 16.5 and Chapter 10 of Division 7 of Title 2 of the California Code of Regulations or use an algorithm approved by the National Institute of Standards and Technology.

- Be unique to the person using it.

- Be under the exclusive control of the individual using it.

- Be linked to the data in such a way that if the data are changed, the signature is invalidated.

- Persist with the electronic document and not by association in separate files.

- Be bound to a digital certificate.

The principal electronically signing a durable power of attorney for health care must leave his or her right thumbprint in the Notary's journal.

Confidential Marriage Certificates

Restrictions. Only specially screened Notaries may issue and notarize confidential marriage certificates. To receive such authorization, a Notary must file an application and a $300 annual fee with the county clerk of the county in which the Notary lives.

After an applicant has undergone a background check and a two-hour course of instruction, the county clerk may issue an authorization for the Notary to execute these certificates. This authorization requires annual renewal (Family Code, Sections 530–536). Any questions about the procedure should be asked of the county clerk in the county in which the Notary resides.

Certificates and Fees. Blank confidential marriage certificates are provided to authorized Notaries by the county clerk for a fee, which the Notary may charge to the married couple along with the notarial fee for a jurat (Family Code, Section 503).

Cannot Perform Marriages. Although a California Notary may issue and notarize confidential marriage certificates, the Notary cannot perform the actual marriage ceremony unless he or she is a religious or civil official authorized to solemnize marriages.

Homeowner's Association Elections

Authority. Notaries are authorized as an independent third party to inspect and guarantee the integrity of a homeowner's association election, provided the Notary is not: a member of, or candidate for, the board of directors; related to a member of, or candidate for, the board of directors; or currently employed or under contract to the association for paid services, unless expressly authorized by the rules of the association (Civil Code, Section 1363.03).

Electronic Signatures

Recognized by State. California's *Uniform Electronic Transactions Act* (UETA) recognizes that electronic signatures may be used with the same legal effect as pen-and-ink signatures, and also recognizes their use by Notaries in performing electronic notarial acts (Civil Code, Section 1633.11).

Digital Signatures. A digital signature is a particular kind of electronic signature created through "public key cryptography," with the following attributes (Government Code, Section 16.5):

- Unique to the person using it

- Capable of verification

- Under the sole control of the person using it

- Linked to data in such a manner that if the data is changed, the digital signature is invalidated

Electronic Real Property Documents. Beginning September 21, 2004, certain "digital documents" — documents created, generated, signed, notarized and transmitted electronically — will require signing parties and Notaries to use electronic signatures to execute these forms. Under law, Notaries may notarize digital reconveyance instruments, substitutions of trustee and assignments of deeds of trust without affixing a physical Notary seal image to the form, as long as the information contained in the Notary seal is included with the Notary's electronic signature. After the notarization is complete, the digital document may be electronically recorded in any California county if the county's electronic recording system has been certified by the Attorney General (Government Code, Section 27391).

MISCONDUCT, FINES AND PENALTIES

Misconduct

Application Misstatement. Substantial and material misstatement or omission in the application for a Notary commission is reason for the Secretary of State to revoke, suspend or refuse to grant a Notary commission (Government Code, Section 8214.1).

Notary's Own Signature. A Notary is not permitted to notarize his or her own signature (Government Code, Section 8224.1).

Felony Conviction. Conviction for a felony or any offense involving moral turpitude or of a nature incompatible with notarial duties, such as forgery, is reason for the Secretary of State to revoke, suspend or refuse to grant a Notary commission. Pleading *nolo contendere* (no contest) is considered a conviction (Government Code, Section 8214.1).

Professional Misconduct. Revocation, suspension, restriction or denial of a professional license for misconduct, dishonesty or any cause substantially relating to notarial duties or responsibilities is reason for the Secretary of State to revoke, suspend or refuse to grant a Notary commission (Government Code, Section 8214.1).

Failure of Duty. Failure to fully and faithfully discharge the duties or responsibilities of a Notary, such as failing to keep a journal of notarial acts, is reason for the Secretary of State to refuse to grant or to revoke or suspend a Notary commission. If the failure is due to negligence, the Secretary may impose a fine of up to $750. If the failure is willful (deliberate and intentional), the Secretary may impose a fine of up to $1,500 (Government Code, Sections 8214.1 and 8214.15).

<u>Falsely Acting as a Notary</u>. Any person not commissioned as a Notary who represents him- or herself, advertises or acts as a Notary is guilty of a misdemeanor (Government Code, Section 8227.1).

Any non-Notary who represents him- or herself as a Notary in relation to any document affecting title to, or placing an encumbrance or interest secured by a mortgage or trust deed on, real property of certain single-family residences is guilty of a felony and may have an application for a Notary commission denied or a commission suspended or revoked (Government Code, Section 8227.3).

<u>Making False Statements to Notary</u>. Any person who knowingly makes a false sworn statement to a Notary, to induce the Notary to perform improper notarizations with regard to the type of real property documents described above, is guilty of a felony and may have an application for a Notary commission denied or a commission suspended or revoked (Government Code, Section 8214.1[b] and Penal Code, Section 115.5[b]).

<u>False or Misleading Advertising</u>. The use of false or misleading advertising by a Notary to represent that he or she has duties, rights and privileges not given by law may subject the Notary to a $1,500 civil penalty and is reason for the Secretary of State to revoke, suspend or refuse to grant a Notary commission (Government Code, Sections 8214.1 and 8214.15).

<u>Improper Foreign-Language Advertising</u>. For failing to include in the advertisement, in English and the foreign language, the statement, "I am not an attorney and, therefore, cannot give legal advice about immigration or any other legal matters," for not including the fees a Notary is allowed to charge or for including a literal Spanish translation of the words "Notary Public" (*Notario Publico* or *Notaria Publica*), a Notary's commission must be revoked or suspended for one year. On the second offense, it must be revoked permanently. In addition, a $1,500 civil penalty may be imposed (Government Code, Sections 8214.1, 8214.15 and 8219.5 and Business and Professions Code, Section 22442.3).

In addition, a non-attorney Notary who literally translates the words "Notary Public" into Spanish will be subject to a civil penalty not to exceed $1,000 per day for each violation to be assessed and collected in a civil action brought by the California State Bar (Business and Professions Code, Section 6126.7).

Advertising as Immigration Expert. No person who claims to be an immigration expert or counselor may also advertise as a Notary Public. This provision is designed to prevent immigration counselors from misrepresenting their powers to unsuspecting foreigners. Violation of the law relating to immigration matters and advertising is reason for the Secretary of State to revoke, suspend or refuse to grant a Notary commission and subjects the Notary to a $1,500 civil penalty (Government Code, Sections 8214.1, 8214.15 and 8223 and Business and Professions Code, Section 22442.3).

Acting as Immigration Consultant without Bond. A Notary may have a commission denied, suspended or revoked and be liable for a $1,500 civil penalty for entering data onto an immigration form or otherwise acting as an immigration consultant without being qualified and bonded as an immigration consultant (Government Code, Sections 8214.1 and 8223).

Unauthorized Practice of Law. The unauthorized practice of law — giving advice on legal matters when one is not a lawyer — is reason for the Secretary of State to deny, revoke or suspend a Notary's commission (Government Code, Section 8214.1 and Business and Professions Code, Section 6125).

Overcharging. Charging more than the maximum fees is reason for the Secretary of State to revoke, suspend or refuse to grant a Notary commission. In addition, a fine of up to $750 may be imposed (Government Code, Sections 8214.1 and 8214.15).
A Notary who charges more than $10 per individual for a set of forms for entering data on immigration forms at the direction of a client may be fined up to $1,500 and have his or her commission denied, suspended or revoked (Government Code, Section 8223).

Dishonesty or Fraud. Committing an act involving dishonesty, fraud or deceit with the intent to substantially benefit the Notary or another, or to substantially injure another, is reason for the Secretary of State to revoke, suspend or refuse to grant a Notary commission. In addition, a fine of up to $1,500 may be imposed (Government Code, Sections 8214.1 and 8214.15).

Intent to Defraud — Real Property. Any Notary who knowingly and willfully performs a notarial act with intent to defraud in relation to a deed of trust on real property (no more than four dwelling units), with knowledge that the deed contains false information or is forged, is guilty of a felony. Committing this offense also is grounds for the Secretary of State to deny, suspend or revoke the Notary's commission (Government Code, Sections 8214.1[b] and 8214.2).

Recording False Instruments. Commission denial, revocation or suspension may occur to anyone who knowingly procures or offers any false or forged instruments to be filed, registered or recorded in any public office in California that, if genuine, might be filed or recorded. Furthermore, any person who knowingly records a false or forged document for real property as described above, in addition to other penalties, may be fined up to $75,000 (Government Code, Section 8214.1 and Penal Code, Section 115 and 115.5).

Found Liable for Fraud. Being found guilty of fraud, misrepresentation or violation of state laws, and being ordered to pay damages, is reason for the Secretary of State to revoke, suspend or deny a Notary's commission (Government Code, Section 8214.1).

Incomplete Acknowledgment. Failure to complete an acknowledgment at the same time the Notary signs and seals the Notary certificate on a document is reason for the Secretary of State to revoke, suspend or refuse to grant a Notary commission. In addition, a fine of up to $750 may be imposed (Government Code, Sections 8214.1 and 8214.15).

False Certificate or Writing. A Notary who knowingly completes a certificate or executes a writing containing statements the Notary knows are false may be charged with a misdemeanor. A misdemeanor charge may be brought within four years after discovery of the violation, or within four years after completion of the offense, whichever is later (Government Code, Section 6203).

Furthermore, a Notary may have his or her commission revoked for executing a certificate containing information the Notary knows is false and may be fined up to $1,500 (Government Code, Section 8214.1)

In addition, any Notary who knowingly completes a false acknowledgment certificate may be charged with forgery (Penal Code, Section 470).

Finally, a Notary who willfully states as true any material fact that he or she knows is false may be fined up to $10,000. This penalty may be imposed by the Secretary of State in an administrative hearing or by a public prosecutor in superior court (Civil Code, Section 1189).

Misuse of Personal Information. The Secretary of State may deny an application or suspend or revoke the commission of a Notary who willfully and unlawfully obtains, retains, sells or uses the personal identifying information of another person to obtain goods or services; commits a crime; or commits mail theft as defined under Penal Code Section 530.5 (Government Code, Section 8214.1[q]).

Failure to Report Loss or Theft of Journal. Willful failure on the part of a Notary to report the loss or theft of his or her journal is is punishable as a misdemeanor and is grounds for the Secretary of State to deny, revoke or suspend a Notary commission (Government Code, Section 8228.1).

Grand Theft. Committing grand theft as defined under Penal Code Sections 487 and 487a(a) is grounds for the Secretary of State to refuse to grant, revoke or suspend a Notary commission (Government Code, Section 8214.1).

Unlawful Influence. Soliciting, coercing or influencing a Notary to perform an improper notarial act, knowing the act to be improper, is punishable as a misdemeanor and is grounds for the Secretary of State to deny, revoke or suspend a Notary commission.

Failure to Provide Journal Access. Willful failure to provide journal access to a peace officer, as defined under Penal Code Sections 830.1, 830.2 and 830.3, is grounds for the Secretary of State to refuse to grant, revoke or suspend a Notary commission. In addition, the Notary may be subject to a $2,500 civil penalty. This penalty may be brought by the Secretary of State in an administrative hearing or by a public prosecutor in superior court (Government Code, Sections 8214.1 and 8214.21).

Failure to Obtain ID for Credible Witness. If a Notary fails to require a personally known credible identifying witness to produce a state-approved ID document, the Notary may incur a civil penalty of up to $10,000. This penalty may be brought by the Secretary of State in an administrative hearing or by a public prosecutor in superior court (Civil Code, Section 1185[b][1][B]).

Failure to Obtain Journal Thumbprint. A Notary who fails to obtain a thumbprint in the journal for a power of attorney, deed, quitclaim deed, deed of trust or other document affecting real property may be fined up to $2,500. The fine may be brought by the Secretary of State in an administrative hearing or by a public prosecutor in superior court (Government Code, Section 8214.23).

False Statement on Immigration Document. It is a misdemeanor for any person, knowingly and for payment, to make a false statement on a document related to immigration. The punishment may be imprisonment in the county jail for a maximum of six months, a fine not exceeding $2,500 or both (Penal Code, Section 653.55).

Oath or Affirmation Not Administered. Failure to administer any oath or affirmation as required by law is reason for the Secretary of State to revoke, suspend or refuse to grant a Notary commission. In addition, a fine of up to $750 may be imposed (Government Code, Sections 8214.1 and 8214.15).

Journal Not Delivered. If a Notary fails or refuses to deliver notarial records to the county clerk, the Notary is guilty of a misdemeanor and is liable for damages suffered by any person as a result (Government Code, Section 8209).

Failure to Secure Journal or Seal. A Notary's failure to keep the official journal and seal in a locked and secured area may result in revocation or suspension of the Notary's commission (Government Code, Section 8214.1).

Misuse of Signature, Seal or Acknowledgment. Any person who, with intent to defraud, forges or counterfeits a Notary signature, seal or acknowledgment of a Notary, or issues an acknowledgment known by the Notary to be false, is guilty of forgery, which is punishable by imprisonment for up to one year (Penal Code, Sections 470, 472 and 473).

Use of Seal for Endorsement or Testimonial. The Notary seal may only be used to carry out the official duties of a Notary Public. Notaries may not use the official seal to endorse or promote any product, service or contest (Government Code, Section 8207).

Failure to Report a Lost or Damaged Seal. Failure to report that a seal is lost, misplaced, destroyed, broken, damaged or otherwise unworkable can result in a $1,500 fine (Government Code, Sections 8207.3 and 8207.4).

Certificate of Authorization Procedure Violation. The failure of a Notary or vendor to comply with procedures regarding the Certificate of Authorization in purchasing or selling a Notary seal can result in a $1,500 fine for each violation. Such a penalty would result from a civil lawsuit initiated by the state attorney general or a local district attorney, city attorney or prosecutor (Government Code, Sections 8207.2, 8207.3 and 8207.4).

Non-payment of Judgment. Failure to submit any remittance to the Secretary of State or to satisfy any court-ordered money judgment, including restitution, is reason for the Secretary of State to revoke, suspend or refuse to grant a Notary commission (Government Code, Section 8214.1).

Delinquency on Child Support Payments. The Secretary of State is prohibited from issuing or renewing a Notary commission for any person who has not complied with child support orders. Any commission fees that have been paid by the applicant will not be refunded (Welfare and Institutions Code, Section 11350.6).

Dishonored Check. The Secretary of State may cancel the commission of a Notary Public if any of the commission fees are not paid due to a returned check. Upon receiving notice from a financial institution that the check or draft was not honored, the Secretary of State will give written notice to the applicant requesting payment by cashier's check. Should the Secretary of State need to issue a second notice, the commission will be cancelled effective the date of that second notice (Government Code, Section 8204.1).

Violating State-Approved Education Requirements. Any person who provides Notary education and violates any regulations the

Secretary of State adopts is subject to a maximum $1,000 fine for each violation and other appropriate damages (Government Code, Section 8201.2).

<u>Willful Failure Regarding Journal and Seal</u>. A Notary who willfully fails to properly maintain a journal of official acts, fails to keep the seal under his or her direct and exclusive control, or surrenders the seal to any person not authorized to possess it is guilty of a misdemeanor. A violation may be prosecuted within four years after discovery of the offense or within four years after completion of the offense, whichever is later (Government Code, Section 8228.1).

<u>Criminal Conviction</u>. Upon conviction for any criminal offense for notarial misconduct, or for any felony, in addition to any other penalty levied, a Notary's commission will be revoked by the court. The Notary must surrender his or her seal of office to the court, who will forward it, along with a certified copy of the judgment of conviction, to the Secretary of State (Government Code, Section 8214.8).

Statute of Limitations

<u>Civil Actions</u>. An action against a Notary's bond or the Notary, while acting in his or her official capacity, must commence within three years from performance of the act.

In cases of misfeasance and malfeasance, an action may commence within three years from performance of the act or within one year of discovery of the act. "Misfeasance" means a lawful act performed in an unlawful manner. An example would be performing a notarization (lawful act) without the signer present (in an unlawful manner). "Malfeasance" means a wrongful act performed by a public official. An example would be notarizing after the commission had expired.

However, an action must be finally brought within six years in cases when malfeasance or misfeasance by the Notary is the grounds for the lawsuit (Code of Civil Procedure, Section 338[f]).

<u>Certain Criminal Acts</u>. The following criminal offenses may be prosecuted within four years after discovery of the offense, or within four years after completion of the offense, whichever is later:

- Making or delivering as true any certificate or writing containing statements known by the Notary to be false (Government Code, Section 6203)

- Failing to obtain a journal thumbprint for the documents for which such thumbprint is required by law (Government Code, Section 8214.23)

- Knowingly destroying, defacing or concealing any records or papers belonging to a Notary (Government Code, Section 8221)

- Improperly soliciting, influencing or coercing a Notary to perform an improper notarial act (Government Code, Section 8225)

- Failing to perform any duty in Government Code 8206 related to the Notary's seal, willfully failing to keep the seal under the Notary's exclusive control or surrendering the seal to any person not otherwise authorized by law to possess the seal (Government Code, Section 8228.1)

Right to a Hearing

<u>Revocation, Suspension or Denial</u>. Before a commission can be revoked or suspended, or after a commission is denied, the Notary or applicant has the right to a hearing. There is one exception, however. When it has been established within one year prior to application for renewal of a Notary's commission that the Notary has committed acts that would result in commission suspension or revocation, the Notary has no right to a hearing (Government Code, Section 8214.3).

<u>Resignation Will Not Stop Investigation</u>. If a Notary under investigation should resign or let his or her commission expire, the Secretary of State may still press the investigation and/or disciplinary proceedings. A record will then be made indicating whether the findings would have caused commission suspension or revocation (Government Code, Section 8214.4).

<u>Filed with County Clerk</u>. When a Notary's commission is revoked, a copy of the revocation is filed by the Secretary of State with the county clerk of the county where the Notary has filed an

oath and bond. The county clerk then notes the revocation and the revocation date in the clerk's official records (Government Code, Section 8214.5). ■

California Laws Pertaining to Notaries Public

Reprinted on the following pages are pertinent sections of California statutes affecting Notaries and notarial acts, mostly drawn from the California Government Code and Civil Code.

CALIFORNIA STATUTES

Government Code

§ 16.5. (a) In any written communication with a public entity, as defined in Section 811.2, in which a signature is required or used, any party to the communication may affix a signature by use of a digital signature that complies with the requirements of this section. The use of a digital signature shall have the same force and effect as the use of a manual signature if and only if it embodies all of the following attributes:

(1) It is unique to the person using it.

(2) It is capable of verification.

(3) It is under the sole control of the person using it.

(4) It is linked to data in such a manner that if the data are changed, the digital signature is invalidated.

(5) It conforms to regulations adopted by the Secretary of State. Initial regulations shall be adopted no later than January 1, 1997. In developing these regulations, the secretary shall seek the advice of public and private entities, including, but not limited to, the Department of Information Technology, the California Environmental Protection Agency, and the Department of General Services. Before the secretary adopts the regulations, he or she shall hold at least one public hearing to receive comments.

(b) The use or acceptance of a digital signature shall be at the option of the parties. Nothing in this section shall require a public entity to use or permit the use of a digital signature.

(c) Digital signatures employed pursuant to Section 71066 of the Public Resources Code are exempted from this section.

(d) "Digital signature" means an electronic identifier, created by computer, intended by the party using it to have the same force and effect as the use of a manual signature.

§ 6100. Officers of the state, or of a county or judicial district, shall not perform any official services unless upon the payment of the fees prescribed by law for the performance of the services, except as provided in this chapter.

This section shall not be construed to prohibit any notary public, except a notary public whose fees are required by law to be remitted to the state or any other public agency, from performing notarial services without charging a fee.

§ 6107. (a) No public entity, including the state, a county, city, or other political subdivision, nor any officer or employee thereof, including notaries public, shall demand or receive any fee or compensation for doing any of the following:

(1) Recording, indexing, or issuing certified copies of any discharge, certificate of service, certificate of satisfactory service, notice of separation, or report of separation of any member of the armed forces of the United States.

(2) Furnishing a certified copy of, or searching for, any public record that is to be used in an application or claim for a pension, allotment, allowance, compensation, insurance (including automatic insurance), or any other benefits under any act of Congress for service in the Armed Forces of the United States or under any law of this state relating to veterans' benefits.

(3) Furnishing a certified copy of, or searching for, any public record that is required by the Veterans Administration to be used in determining the eligibility of any person to participate in benefits made available by the Veterans Administration.

(4) Rendering any other service in connection with an application or claim referred to in paragraph (2) or (3).

(b) A certified copy of any record referred to in subdivision (a) may be made available only to one of the following:

(1) The person who is the subject of the record upon presentation of proper photo identification.

(2) A family member or legal representative of the person who is the subject of the record upon presentation of proper photo identification and certification of their relationship to the subject of the record.

(3) A county office that provides veteran's benefits services upon written request of that office.

(4) A United States official upon written request of that official. A public officer or employee is liable on his or her official bond for failure or refusal to render the services.

§ 6109. Every officer of a county or judicial district, upon receiving any fees for official duty or service, may be required by the person paying the fees to make out in writing and to deliver to the person a particular account of the fees. The account shall specify for what the fees, respectively, accrued, and the officer shall receipt it. If the officer refuses or neglects to do so when required, he is liable to the person paying the fees in treble the amount so paid.

§ 6110. Upon payment of the fees required by law, the officer shall perform the services required. For every failure or refusal to do so, the officer is liable upon his official bond.

§ 6203. (a) Every officer authorized by law to make or give any certificate or other writing is guilty of a misdemeanor if he or she makes and delivers as true any certificate or writing containing statements which he or she knows to be false.

(b) Notwithstanding any other limitation of time described in Section 802 of the Penal Code, or any other provision of law, prosecution for a violation of this offense shall be commenced within four years after discovery of the commission of the offense, or within four years after the completion of the offense, whichever is later.

(c) The penalty provided by this section is not an exclusive remedy, and does not affect any other relief or remedy provided by law.

§ 8200. The Secretary of State may appoint and commission notaries public in such number as the Secretary of State deems necessary for the public convenience. Notaries public may act as such notaries in any part of this state.

§ 8201. (a) Every person appointed as notary public shall meet all of the following requirements:

(1) Be at the time of appointment a legal resident of this state, except as otherwise provided in Section 8203.1.

(2) Be not less than 18 years of age.

(3) For appointments made on or after January 1, 2005, have satisfactorily completed a six-hour course of study approved by the Secretary of State pursuant to Section 8201.2 concerning the functions and duties of a notary public.

(4) Have satisfactorily completed a written examination prescribed by the Secretary of State to determine the fitness of the person to exercise the functions of the office of notary public. All questions shall be based on the law of this state as set forth in the booklet of the laws of California relating to notaries public distributed by the Secretary of State.

(b) (1) Commencing July 1, 2005, each applicant for notary public shall provide satisfactory proof that he or she has completed the course of study required pursuant to paragraph (3) of subdivision (a) prior to approval of his or her appointment by the Secretary of State.

(2) Commencing July 1, 2005, an applicant for notary public who holds a California notary public commission, and who has satisfactorily completed the six-hour course of study pursuant to paragraph (1) at least one time, shall provide satisfactory proof that he or she has satisfactorily completed a three-hour refresher course of study prior to reappointment as a notary public by the Secretary of State.

§ 8201.1. (a) Prior to granting an appointment as a notary public, the Secretary of State shall determine that the applicant possesses the required honesty, credibility, truthfulness, and integrity to fulfill the responsibilities of the position. To assist in determining the identity of the applicant and whether the applicant has been convicted of a disqualifying crime specified in subdivision (b) of Section 8214.1, the Secretary of State shall require that applicants be fingerprinted.

(b) Applicants shall submit to the Department of Justice fingerprint images and related information required by the department for the purpose of obtaining information as to the existence and content of a record of state and federal convictions and arrests and information as to the existence and content of a record of state and federal arrests for which the department establishes that the person is free on bail, or on his or her recognizance, pending trial or appeal.

(c) The department shall forward the fingerprint images and related information received pursuant to subdivision (a) to the Federal Bureau of Investigation and request a federal summary of criminal information.

(d) The department shall review the information returned from the Federal Bureau of Investigation and compile and disseminate a response to the Secretary of State pursuant to paragraph (1) of subdivision (p) of Section 11105 of the Penal Code.

(e) The Secretary of State shall request from the department subsequent arrest notification service, pursuant to Section 11105.2 of the Penal Code, for each person who submitted information pursuant to subdivision (a).

(f) The department shall charge a fee sufficient to cover the cost of processing the requests described in this section.

§ 8201.2. (a) The Secretary of State shall review the course of study proposed by any vendor to be offered pursuant to paragraph (3) of subdivision (a) and paragraph (2) of subdivision (b) of Section 8201. If the course of study includes all material that a person is expected to know to satisfactorily complete the written examination required pursuant to paragraph (4) of subdivision (a) of Section 8201, the Secretary of State shall approve the course of study.

(b) (1) The Secretary of State shall, by regulation, prescribe an application form and adopt a certificate of approval for the notary public education course of study proposed by a vendor.

(2) The Secretary of State may also provide a notary public education course of study.

(c) The Secretary of State shall compile a list of all persons offering an approved course of study pursuant to subdivision (a) and shall provide the list with every booklet of the laws of California relating to notaries public distributed by the Secretary of State.

(d) (1) A person who provides notary public education and violates any of the regulations adopted by the Secretary of State for approved vendors is subject to a civil penalty not to exceed one thousand dollars ($1,000) for each violation and shall be required to pay restitution where appropriate.

(2) The local district attorney, city attorney, or the Attorney General may bring a civil action to recover the civil penalty prescribed pursuant to this subdivision. A public prosecutor shall inform the Secretary of State of any civil penalty imposed under this section.

§ 8201.5. The Secretary of State shall require an applicant for appointment and commission as a notary public to complete an application form and submit a photograph of their person as prescribed by the Secretary of State. Information on this form filed by an applicant with the Secretary of State, except for his or her name and address, is confidential and no individual record shall be divulged by an official or employee having access to it to any person other than the applicant, his or her authorized representative, or an employee or officer of the federal government, the state government, or a local agency, as defined in subdivision (b) of Section 6252 of the Government Code, acting in his or her official capacity. That information shall be used by the Secretary of State for the sole purpose of carrying out the duties of this chapter.

§ 8202. (a) When executing a jurat, a notary shall administer an oath or affirmation to the affiant and shall determine, from satisfactory evidence as described in Section 1185 of the Civil Code, that the affiant is the person executing the document. The affiant shall sign the document in the presence of the notary.

(b) To any affidavit subscribed and sworn to before a notary, there shall be attached a jurat that includes a notice at the top, in an enclosed box, stating: "A notary public or other officer completing this certificate verifies only the identity of the individual who signed the document to which this certificate is attached, and not the truthfulness, accuracy, or validity of that document." This notice shall be legible.

(c) The physical format of the boxed notice at the top of the jurat required pursuant to subdivision (d) is an example, for purposes of illustration and not limitation, of the physical format of a boxed notice fulfilling the requirements of subdivision (b).

(d) A jurat executed pursuant to this section shall be in the following form:

> A notary public or other officer completing this certificate verifies only the identity of the individual who signed the document to which this certificate is attached, and not the truthfulness, accuracy, or validity of that document.

State of California
County of _____

Subscribed and sworn to (or affirmed) before me on this _____ day of _____, 20__, by _____, proved to me on the basis of satisfactory evidence to be the person(s) who appeared before me.

Signature   (Seal)

§ 8202.5. The Secretary of State may appoint and commission the number of state, city, county, and public school district employees as notaries public to act for and on behalf of the governmental entity for which appointed which the Secretary of State deems proper. Whenever a notary is appointed and commissioned, a duly authorized representative of the employing governmental entity shall execute a certificate that the appointment is made for the purposes of the employing governmental entity, and whenever the certificate is filed with any state or county officer, no fees shall be charged by the officer for the filing or issuance of any document in connection with the appointment. The state or any city, county, or school district for which the notary public is appointed and commissioned pursuant to this section may pay from any funds available for its support the premiums on any bond and the cost of any stamps, seals, or other supplies required in connection with the appointment, commission, or performance of the duties of the notary public.

Any fees collected or obtained by any notary public whose documents have been filed without charge and for whom bond premiums have been paid by the employer of the notary public shall be remitted by the notary public to the employing agency which shall deposit the funds to the credit of the fund from which the salary of the notary public is paid.

§ 8202.7. A private employer, pursuant to an agreement with an employee who is a notary public, may pay the premiums on any bond and the cost of any stamps, seals, or other supplies required in connection with the appointment, commission, or performance of the duties of such notary public. Such agreement may also provide for the remission of fees collected by such notary public to the employer, in which case any fees collected or obtained by such notary public while such agreement is in effect shall be remitted by such notary public to the employer which shall deposit such funds to the credit of the fund from which the compensation of the notary public is paid.

§ 8202.8. Notwithstanding any other provision of law, a private employer of a notary public who has entered into an agreement with his or her employee pursuant to Section 8202.7 may limit, during the employee's ordinary course of employment, the providing of notarial services by the employee solely to transactions directly associated with the business purposes of the employer.

§ 8203.1. The Secretary of State may appoint and commission notaries public for the military and naval reservations of the Army, Navy, Coast Guard, Air Force, and Marine Corps of the United States, wherever located in the state; provided, however, that the appointee shall be a citizen of the United States, not less than 18 years of age, and must meet the requirements set forth in paragraphs (3) and (4) of subdivision (a) of Section 8201.

§ 8203.2. Such notaries public shall be appointed only upon the recommendation of the commanding officer of the reservation in which they are to act, and they shall be authorized to act only within the boundaries of this reservation.

§ 8203.3. In addition to the qualifications established in Section 8203.1, appointment will be made only from among those persons who are federal civil service employees at the reservation in which they will act as notaries public.

§ 8203.4. The term of office shall be as set forth in Section 8204, except that the appointment shall terminate if the person shall cease to be employed as a federal civil service employee at the reservation for which appointed. The commanding officer of the reservation shall notify the Secretary of State of termination of employment at the reservation for which appointed within 30 days of such termination. A notary public whose appointment terminates pursuant to this section will have such termination treated as a resignation.

§ 8203.5. In addition to the name of the State, the jurat shall also contain the name of the reservation in which the instrument is executed.

§ 8203.6. No fees shall be collected by such notaries public for service rendered within the reservation in the capacity of a notary public.

§ 8204. The term of office of a notary public is for four years commencing with the date specified in the commission.

§ 8204.1. The Secretary of State may cancel the commission of a notary public if a check or other remittance accepted as payment for the examination, application, commission, and fingerprint fee is not paid upon presentation to the financial institution upon which the check or other remittance was drawn. Upon receiving written notification that the item presented for payment has not been honored for payment, the Secretary of State shall first give a written notice of the applicability of this section to the notary public or the person submitting the instrument. Thereafter, if the amount is not paid by a cashier's check or the equivalent, the Secretary of State shall give a second written notice of cancellation and the cancellation shall thereupon be effective. This second notice shall be given at least 20 days after the first notice, and no more than 90 days after the commencement date of the commission.

§ 8205. (a) It is the duty of a notary public, when requested: (1) To demand acceptance and payment of foreign and inland bills of exchange, or promissory notes, to protest them for nonacceptance and nonpayment, and, with regard only to the nonacceptance or nonpayment of bills and notes, to exercise any other powers and duties that by the law of nations and according to commercial usages, or by the laws of any other state, government, or country, may be performed by a notary. This paragraph applies only to a notary public employed by a financial institution, during the course and scope of the notary's employment with the financial institution.

(2) To take the acknowledgment or proof of advance health care directives, powers of attorney, mortgages, deeds, grants, transfers, and other instruments of writing executed by any person, and to give a certificate of that proof or acknowledgment, endorsed on or attached to the instrument. The certificate shall be signed by the notary public in the notary public's own handwriting. A notary public may not accept any acknowledgment or proof of any instrument that is incomplete.

(3) To take depositions and affidavits, and administer oaths and affirmations, in all matters incident to the duties of the office, or to be used before any court, judge, officer, or board. Any deposition, affidavit, oath, or affirmation shall be signed by the notary public in the notary public's own handwriting.

(4) To certify copies of powers of attorney under Section 4307 of the Probate Code. The certification shall be signed by the notary public in the notary public's own handwriting.

(b) It shall further be the duty of a notary public, upon written request:

(1) To furnish to the Secretary of State certified copies of the notary's journal.

(2) To respond within 30 days of receiving written requests sent by certified mail from the Secretary of State's office for information relating to official acts performed by the notary.

§ 8206. (a) (1) A notary public shall keep one active sequential journal at a time, of all official acts performed as a notary public. The journal shall be kept in a locked and secured area, under the direct and exclusive control of the notary. Failure to secure the journal shall be cause for the Secretary of State to take administrative action against the commission held by the notary public pursuant to Section 8214.1.

(2) The journal shall be in addition to, and apart from, any copies of notarized documents that may be in the possession of the notary public and shall include all of the following:

(A) Date, time, and type of each official act.

(B) Character of every instrument sworn to, affirmed, acknowledged, or proved before the notary.

(C) The signature of each person whose signature is being notarized.

(D) A statement as to whether the identity of a person making an acknowledgment or taking an oath or affirmation was based on satisfactory evidence. If identity was established by satisfactory evidence pursuant to Section 1185 of the Civil Code, the journal shall contain the signature of the credible witness swearing or affirming to the identity of the individual or the type of identifying document, the governmental agency issuing the document, the serial or identifying number of the document, and the date of issue or expiration of the document.

(E) If the identity of the person making the acknowledgment or taking the oath or affirmation was established by the oaths or affirmations of two credible witnesses whose identities are proven to the notary public by presentation of any document satisfying the requirements of paragraph (3) or (4) of subdivision (b) of Section 1185 of the Civil Code, the notary public shall record in the journal the type of documents identifying the witnesses, the identifying numbers on the documents identifying the witnesses, and the dates of issuance or expiration of the documents presented identifying the witnesses.

(F) The fee charged for the notarial service.

(G) If the document to be notarized is a deed, quitclaim deed, deed of trust or other document affecting real property, or a power of attorney document, the notary public shall require the party signing the document to place his or her right thumbprint in the journal. If the right thumbprint is not available, then the notary shall have the party use his or her left thumb, or any available finger and shall so indicate in the journal. If the party signing the document is physically unable to provide a thumbprint or fingerprint, the notary shall so indicate in the journal and shall also provide an explanation of that physical condition. This paragraph shall not apply to a trustee's deed resulting from a decree of foreclosure or a nonjudicial foreclosure pursuant to Section 2924 of the Civil Code, nor to a deed of reconveyance.

(b) If a sequential journal of official acts performed by a notary public is stolen, lost, misplaced, destroyed, damaged, or otherwise rendered unusable as a record of notarial acts and information, the notary public shall immediately notify the Secretary of State by certified or registered mail. The notification shall include the period of the journal entries, the notary public commission number, and the expiration date of the commission, and when applicable, a photocopy of any police report that specifies the theft of the sequential journal of official acts.

(c) Upon written request of any member of the public, which request shall include the name of the parties, the type of document, and the month and year in which notarized, the notary shall supply a photostatic copy of the line item representing the requested transaction at a cost of not more than thirty cents ($0.30) per page.

(d) The journal of notarial acts of a notary public is the exclusive property of that notary public, and shall not be surrendered to an employer upon termination of employment, whether or not the employer paid for the journal, or at any other time. The notary public shall not surrender the journal to any other person, except the county clerk, pursuant to Section 8209, or immediately, or if the journal is not present then as soon as possible, upon request to a peace officer investigating a criminal offense who has reasonable suspicion to believe the journal contains evidence of a criminal offense, as defined in Sections 830.1, 830.2, and 830.3 of the Penal Code, acting in his or her official capacity and within his or her authority. If the peace officer seizes the notary journal, he or she must have probable cause as required by the laws of this state and the United States. A peace officer or law enforcement agency that seizes a notary journal shall notify the Secretary of State by facsimile within 24 hours, or as soon possible thereafter, of the name of the notary public whose journal has been seized. The notary public shall obtain a receipt for the journal, and shall notify the Secretary of State by certified mail within 10 days that the journal was relinquished to a peace officer. The notification shall include the period of the journal entries, the commission number of the notary public, the expiration date of the commission, and a photocopy of the receipt. The notary public shall obtain a new sequential journal. If the journal relinquished to a peace officer is returned to the notary public and a new journal has been obtained, the notary public shall make no new entries in the returned journal. A notary public who is an employee shall permit inspection and copying of journal transactions by a duly designated auditor or agent of the notary public's employer, provided that the inspection and copying is done in the presence of the notary public and the transactions are directly associated with the business purposes of the employer. The notary public, upon the request of the employer, shall regularly provide copies of all transactions that are directly associated with the business purposes of the employer, but shall not be required to provide copies of any transaction that is unrelated to the employer's business. Confidentiality and safekeeping of any copies of the journal provided to the employer shall be the responsibility of that employer.

(e) The notary public shall provide the journal for examination and copying in the presence of the notary public upon receipt of a subpoena duces tecum or a court order, and shall certify those copies if requested.

(f) Any applicable requirements of, or exceptions to, state and federal law shall apply to a peace officer engaged in the search or seizure of a sequential journal.

§ 8206.5. Upon receiving a request for a copy of a transaction pursuant to subdivision (c) of Section 8206, the notary shall respond to the request within 15 business days after receipt of the request and either supply the photostatic copy requested or acknowledge that no such line item exists. In a disciplinary proceeding for noncompliance with subdivision (c) of Section 8206 or this section, a notary may defend his or her delayed action on the basis of unavoidable, exigent business or personal circumstances.

§ 8207. A notary public shall provide and keep an official seal, which shall clearly show, when embossed, stamped, impressed or affixed to a document, the name of the notary, the State Seal, the words "Notary Public," and the name of the county wherein the bond and oath of office are filed, and the date the notary public's commission expires. The seal of every notary public commissioned on or after January 1, 1992, shall contain the sequential identification number assigned to the notary and the sequential identification number assigned to the manufacturer or vendor. The notary public shall authenticate with the official seal all official acts. A notary public shall not use the official notarial seal except for the purpose of carrying out the duties and responsibilities as set forth in this chapter. A notary public shall not use the title "notary public" except for the purpose of rendering notarial service.

The seal of every notary public shall be affixed by a seal press or stamp that will print or emboss a seal which legibly reproduces under photographic methods the required elements of the seal. The seal may be circular not over two inches in diameter, or may be a rectangular form of not more than one inch in width by two and one-half inches in length, with a serrated or milled edged border, and shall contain the information required by this section. The seal shall be kept in a locked and secured area, under the direct and exclusive control of the notary. Failure to secure the seal shall be cause for the Secretary of State to take administrative action against the commission held by the notary public pursuant to Section 8214.1.

The official seal of a notary public is the exclusive property of that notary public, and shall not be surrendered to an employer upon the termination of employment, whether or not the employer paid for the seal, or to any other person. The notary, or his or her representative, shall destroy or deface the seal upon termination, resignation, or revocation of the notary's commission.

§ 8207.1. The Secretary of State shall assign a sequential identification number to each notary which shall appear on the notary commission.

§ 8207.2. (a) No notary seal or press stamp shall be manufactured, duplicated, sold, or offered for sale unless authorized by the Secretary of State.

(b) The Secretary of State shall develop and implement procedures and guidelines for the issuance of notary seals on or before January 1, 1992.

(c) The Secretary of State shall issue a permit with a sequential identification number to each manufacturer or vendor authorized to issue notary seals. The Secretary of State may establish a fee for the issuance of the permit which shall not exceed the actual costs of issuing the permit.

(d) The Secretary of State shall develop a certificate of authorization to purchase a notary stamp from an authorized vendor.

(e) The certificate of authorization shall be designed to prevent forgeries and shall contain a sequential identification number.

§ 8207.3. (a) The Secretary of State shall issue certificates of authorization with which a notary public can obtain an official notary seal.

(b) A vendor or manufacturer is authorized to provide a notary with an official seal only upon presentation by the notary public of a certificate of authorization.

(c) A vendor of official seals shall note the receipt of certificates of authorization and sequential identification numbers of certificates presented by a notary public upon a certificate of authorization.

(d) A copy of a certificate of authorization shall be retained by a vendor and the original, which shall contain a sample impression of the seal issued to the notary public, shall be submitted to the Secretary of State for verification and recordkeeping. The Secretary of State shall develop guidelines for submitting certificates of authorization by vendors.

(e) Any notary whose official seal is lost, misplaced, destroyed, broken, damaged, or is rendered otherwise unworkable shall immediately mail or deliver written notice of that fact to the Secretary of State. The Secretary of State, within five working days after receipt of the notice, if requested by a notary, shall issue a certificate of authorization which a notary may use to obtain a replacement seal.

§ 8207.4. (a) Any person who willfully violates any part of Section 8207.1, 8207.2, 8207.3, or 8207.4 shall be subject to a civil penalty not to exceed one thousand five hundred dollars ($1,500) for each violation, which may be recovered in a civil action brought by the Attorney General or the district attorney or city attorney, or by a city prosecutor in any city and county.

(b) The penalty provided by this section is not an exclusive remedy, and does not affect any other relief or remedy provided by law.

§ 8208. The protest of a notary public, acting in the course and scope of employment by a financial institution, under his or her hand and official seal, of a bill of exchange or promissory note for nonacceptance or nonpayment, specifying any of the following is prima facie evidence of the facts recited therein:

(a) The time and place of presentment.

(b) The fact that presentment was made and the manner thereof.

(c) The cause or reason for protesting the bill.

(d) The demand made and the answer given, if any, or the fact that the drawee or acceptor could not be found.

§ 8209. (a) If any notary public resigns, is disqualified, removed from office, or allows his or her appointment to expire without obtaining reappointment within 30 days, all notarial records and papers shall be delivered within 30 days to the clerk of the county in which the notary public's current official oath of office is on file. If the notary public willfully fails or refuses to deliver all notarial records and papers to the county clerk within 30 days, the person is guilty of a misdemeanor and shall be personally liable for damages to any person injured by that action or inaction.

(b) In the case of the death of a notary public, the personal representative of the deceased shall promptly notify the Secretary of State of the death of the notary public and shall deliver all notarial records and papers of the deceased to the clerk of the county in which the notary public's official oath of office is on file.

(c) After 10 years from the date of deposit with the county clerk, if no request for, or reference to such records has been made, they may be destroyed upon order of court.

§ 8211. Fees charged by a notary public for the following services shall not exceed the fees prescribed by this section.

(a) For taking an acknowledgment or proof of a deed, or other instrument, to include the seal and the writing of the certificate, the sum of ten dollars ($10) for each signature taken.

(b) For administering an oath or affirmation to one person and executing the jurat, including the seal, the sum of ten dollars ($10).

(c) For all services rendered in connection with the taking of any deposition, the sum of twenty dollars ($20), and in addition thereto, the sum of five dollars ($5) for administering the oath to the witness and the sum of five dollars ($5) for the certificate to the deposition.

(d) No fee may be charged to notarize signatures on absentee ballot identification envelopes or other voting materials.

(e) For certifying a copy of a power of attorney under Section 4307 of the Probate Code the sum of ten dollars ($10).

(f) In accordance with section 6107, no fee may be charged to a United States military veteran for notarization of an application or a claim for a pension.

(g) No fee may be charged to notarize signatures on absentee ballot identification envelopes or other voting materials.

(h) For certifying a copy of a power of attorney under Section 4307 of the Probate Code the sum of ten dollars ($10).

(i) In accordance with section 6107, no fee may be charged to a United States military veteran for notarization of an application or a claim for a pension allotment, allowance, compensation, insurance, or any other veteran's benefit.

§ 8212. Every person appointed a notary public shall execute an official bond in the sum of fifteen thousand dollars ($15,000). The bond shall be in the form of a bond executed by an admitted surety insurer and not a deposit in lieu of bond.

§ 8213. (a) No later than 30 days after the beginning of the term prescribed in the commission, every person appointed a notary public shall file an official bond and an oath of office in the office of the county clerk of the county within which the person maintains a principal place of business as shown in the application submitted to the Secretary of State, and the commission shall not take effect unless this is done within the 30-day period. A person appointed to be a notary public shall take and subscribe the oath of office either in the office of that county clerk or before another notary public in that county. If the oath of office is taken and subscribed before a notary public, the oath and bond may be filed with the county clerk by certified mail. Upon the filing of the oath and bond, the county clerk shall immediately transmit to the Secretary of State a certificate setting forth the fact of the filing and containing a copy of the official oath, personally signed by the notary public in the form set forth in the commission and shall immediately deliver the bond to the county recorder for recording. The county clerk shall retain the oath of office for one year following the expiration of the term of the commission for which the oath was taken, after which the oath may be destroyed or otherwise disposed of. The copy of the oath, personally signed by the notary public, on file with the Secretary of State may at any time be read in evidence with like effect as the original oath, without further proof.

(b) If a notary public transfers the principal place of business from one county to another, the notary public may file a new oath of office and bond, or a duplicate of the original bond with the county clerk to which the principal place of business was transferred. If the notary public elects to make a new filing, the notary public shall, within 30 days of the filing, obtain an official seal which shall include the name of the county to which the notary public has transferred. In a case where the notary public elects to make a new filing, the same filing and recording fees are applicable as in the case of the original filing and recording of the bond.

(c) If a notary public submits an application for a name change to the Secretary of State, the notary public shall, within 30 days from the date an amended commission is issued, file a new oath of office and an amendment to the bond with the county clerk in which the principal place of business is located. The amended commission with the name change shall not take effect unless the filing is completed within the 30-day period. The amended commission with the name change takes effect the date the oath and amendment to the bond is filed with the county clerk. If the principal place of business address was changed in the application for name change, either a new or duplicate of the original bond shall be filed with the county clerk with the amendment to the bond. The notary public shall, within 30 days of the filing, obtain an official seal that includes the name of the notary public and the name of the county to which the notary public has transferred, if applicable.

(d) The recording fee specified in Section 27361 of the Government Code shall be paid by the person appointed a notary public. The fee may be paid to the county clerk who shall transmit it to the county recorder.

(e) The county recorder shall record the bond and shall thereafter mail, unless specified to the contrary, it to the person named in the instrument and, if no person is named, to the party leaving it for recording.

§ 8213.5. A notary public shall notify the Secretary of State by certified mail within 30 days as to any change in the location or address of the principal place of business or residence. A notary public shall not use a commercial mail receiving agency or post office box as his or her principal place of business or residence, unless the notary public also provides the Secretary of State with a physical street address as the principal place of residence. Willful failure to notify the Secretary of State of a change of address shall be punishable as an infraction by a fine of not more than five hundred dollars ($500).

§ 8213.6. If a notary public changes his or her name, the notary public shall complete an application for name change form and file that application with the Secretary of State. Information on this form shall be subject to the confidentiality provisions described in Section 8201.5. Upon approval of the name change form, the Secretary of State shall issue a commission that reflects the new name of the notary public. The term of the commission and commission number shall remain the same. Willful failure to notify the Secretary of State of a name change shall be punishable as an infraction by a fine of not more than five hundred dollars ($500).

§ 8214. For the official misconduct or neglect of a notary public, the notary public and the sureties on the notary public's official bond are liable in a civil action to the persons injured thereby for all the damages sustained.

§ 8214.1. The Secretary of State may refuse to appoint any person as notary public or may revoke or suspend the commission of any notary public upon any of the following grounds:

(a) Substantial and material misstatement or omission in the application submitted to the Secretary of State to become a notary public.

(b) Conviction of a felony, a lesser offense involving moral turpitude, or a lesser offense of a nature incompatible with the duties of a notary public. A conviction after a plea of nolo contendere is deemed to be a conviction within the meaning of this subdivision.

(c) Revocation, suspension, restriction, or denial of a professional license, if the revocation, suspension, restriction, or denial was for misconduct based on dishonesty, or for any cause substantially relating to the duties or responsibilities of a notary public.

(d) Failure to discharge fully and faithfully any of the duties or responsibilities required of a notary public.

(e) When adjudicated liable for damages in any suit grounded in fraud, misrepresentation, or for a violation of the state regulatory laws, or in any suit based upon a failure to discharge fully and faithfully the duties as a notary public.

(f) The use of false or misleading advertising wherein the notary public has represented that the notary public has duties, rights, or privileges that he or she does not possess by law.

(g) The practice of law in violation of Section 6125 of the Business and Professions Code.

(h) Charging more than the fees prescribed by this chapter.

(i) Commission of any act involving dishonesty, fraud, or deceit with the intent to substantially benefit the notary public or another, or substantially injure another.

(j) Failure to complete the acknowledgment at the time the notary's signature and seal are affixed to the document.

(k) Failure to administer the oath or affirmation as required by paragraph (3) of subdivision (a) of Section 8205.

(l) Execution of any certificate as a notary public containing a statement known to the notary public to be false.

(m) Violation of Section 8223.

(n) Failure to submit any remittance payable upon demand by the Secretary of State under this chapter or failure to satisfy any court-ordered money judgment, including restitution.

(o) Failure to secure the sequential journal of official acts, pursuant to Section 8206, or the official seal, pursuant to Section 8207, or willful failure to report the theft or loss of the sequential journal, pursuant to subdivision (b) of Section 8206.

(p) Violation of Section 8219.5.

(q) Commission of an act in violation of Section 6203, 8214.2, 8225, or 8227.3 of the Government Code or of Section 115, 470, 487, subdivision (a) of Section

487a, or Section 530.5 of the Penal Code.

(r) Willful failure to provide access to the sequential journal of official acts upon request by a peace officer.

§ 8214.15. (a) In addition to any commissioning or disciplinary sanction, a violation of subdivision (f), (i), (l), (m), or (p) of Section 8214.1, or a willful violation of subdivision (d) of Section 8214.1, is punishable by a civil penalty not to exceed one thousand five hundred dollars ($1,500).

(b) In addition to any commissioning or disciplinary sanction, a violation of subdivision (h), (j), or (k) of Section 8214.1, or a negligent violation of subdivision (d) of Section 8214.1 is punishable by a civil penalty not to exceed seven hundred fifty dollars ($750).

(c) The civil penalty may be imposed by the Secretary of State if a hearing is not requested pursuant to Section 8214.3. If a hearing is requested, the hearing officer shall make the determination.

(d) Any civil penalties collected pursuant to this section shall be transferred to the General Fund. It is the intent of the Legislature that to the extent General Fund moneys are raised by penalties collected pursuant to this section, that money shall be made available to the Secretary of State's office to defray its costs of investigating and pursuing commissioning and monetary remedies for violations of the notary public law.

§ 8214.2. (a) A notary public who knowingly and willfully with intent to defraud performs any notarial act in relation to a deed of trust on real property consisting of a single-family residence containing not more than four dwelling units, with knowledge that the deed of trust contains any false statements or is forged, in whole or in part, is guilty of a felony.

(b) The penalty provided by this section is not an exclusive remedy and does not affect any other relief or remedy provided by law.

§ 8214.21. A notary public who willfully fails to provide access to the sequential journal of notarial acts when requested by a peace officer shall be subject to a civil penalty not exceeding two thousand five hundred dollars ($2,500). An action to impose a civil penalty under this subdivision may be brought by the Secretary of State in an administrative proceeding or any public prosecutor in superior court, and shall be enforced as a civil judgment. A public prosecutor shall inform the secretary of any civil penalty imposed under this section.

§ 8214.23. (a) A notary public who fails to obtain a thumbprint, as required by Section 8206, from a party signing a document shall be subject to a civil penalty not exceeding two thousand five hundred dollars ($2,500). An action to impose a civil penalty under this subdivision may be brought by the Secretary of State in an administrative proceeding or any public prosecutor in superior court, and shall be enforced as a civil judgment. A public prosecutor shall inform the secretary of any civil penalty imposed under this section.

(b) Notwithstanding any other limitation of time described in Section 802 of the Penal Code, or any other provision of law, prosecution for a violation of this offense shall be commenced within four years after discovery of the commission of the offense, or within four years after the completion of the offense, whichever is later

§ 8214.3. Prior to a revocation or suspension pursuant to this chapter or after a denial of a commission, or prior to the imposition of a civil penalty, the person affected shall have a right to a hearing on the matter and the proceeding shall be conducted in accordance with Chapter 5 (commencing with Section 11500) of Part 1 of Division 3, except that a person shall not have a right to a hearing after a denial of an application for a notary public commission in either of the following cases:

(a) The Secretary of State has, within one year previous to the application, and after proceedings conducted in accordance with Chapter 5 (commencing with Section 11500) of Part 1 of Division 3, denied or revoked the applicant's application or commission.

(b) The Secretary of State has entered an order pursuant to Section 8214.4 finding that the applicant has committed or omitted acts constituting grounds for suspension or revocation of a notary public's commission.

§ 8214.4. Notwithstanding this chapter or Chapter 5 (commencing with Section 11500) of Part 1 of Division 3, if the Secretary of State determines, after proceedings conducted in accordance with Chapter 5 (commencing with Section 11500) of Part 1 of Division 3, that any notary public has committed or omitted acts constituting grounds for suspension or revocation of a notary public's commission, the resignation or expiration of the notary public's commission shall not bar the Secretary of State from instituting or continuing an investigation or instituting disciplinary proceedings. Upon completion of the disciplinary proceedings, the Secretary of State shall enter an order finding the facts and stating the conclusion that the facts would or would not have constituted grounds for suspension or revocation of the commission if the commission had still been in effect.

§ 8214.5. Whenever the Secretary of State revokes the commission of any notary public, the Secretary of State shall file with the county clerk of the county in which the notary public's principal place of business is located a copy of the revocation. The county clerk shall note such revocation and its date upon the original record of such certificate.

§ 8214.8. Upon conviction of any offense in this chapter, or of section 6203, or of any felony, of a person commissioned as a notary public, in addition to any other penalty, the court shall revoke the commission of the notary public and shall require the notary public to surrender to the court the seal of the notary public. The court shall forward the seal, together with a certified copy of the judgment of conviction, to the Secretary of State.

§ 8216. When a surety of a notary desires to be released from responsibility on account of future acts, the release shall be pursuant to Article 11 (commencing with Section 996.110), and not by cancellation or withdrawal pursuant to Article 13 (commencing with Section 996.310), of Chapter 2 of Title 14 of Part 2 of the Code of Civil Procedure. For this purpose the surety shall make application to the superior court of the county in which the notary public's principal place of business is located and the copy of the application and notice of hearing shall be served on the Secretary of State as the beneficiary.

§ 8219.5. (a) Every notary public who is not an attorney who advertises the services of a notary public in a language other than English by signs or other means of written communication, with the exception of a single desk plaque, shall post with that advertisement a notice in English and in the other language which sets forth the following:

(1) This statement: I am not an attorney and, therefore, cannot give legal advice about immigration or any other legal matters.

(2) The fees set by statute which a notary public may charge.

(b) The notice required by subdivision (a) shall be printed and posted as prescribed by the Secretary of State.

(c) Literal translation of the phrase "notary public" into Spanish, hereby defined as "notario publico" or "notario," is prohibited.***

(d) The Secretary of State shall suspend for a period of not less than one year or revoke the commission of any notary public who fails to comply with subdivision (a) or (c). However, on the second offense the commission of such notary public shall be revoked permanently.

§ 8221. (a) If any person shall knowingly destroy, deface, or conceal any records or papers belonging to the office of a notary public, such person shall be guilty of a misdemeanor and be liable in a civil action for damages to any person injured as a result of such destruction, defacing, or concealment.

(b) Notwithstanding any other limitation of time described in Section 802 of the Penal Code, or any other provision of law, prosecution for a violation of this offense shall be commenced within four years after discovery of the commission of the offense, or within four years after the completion of the offense, whichever is later.

(c) The penalty provided by this section is not an exclusive remedy and does not affect any other relief or remedy provided by law.

§ 8222. (a) Whenever it appears to the Secretary of State that any person has engaged or is about to engage in any acts or practices which constitute or will constitute a violation of any provision of this chapter or any rule or regulation prescribed under the authority thereof, the Secretary of State may apply for an injunction, and upon a proper showing, any court of competent jurisdiction has power to issue a permanent or temporary injunction or restraining order to enforce the provisions of this chapter, and any party to the action has the right to prosecute an appeal from the order or judgment of the court.

(b) The court may order a person subject to an injunction or restraining order provided for in this section to reimburse the Secretary of State for expenses incurred in the investigation related to the petition. The Secretary of State shall refund any amount received as reimbursement should the injunction or restraining order be dissolved by an appellate court.

§ 8223. (a) No notary public who holds himself or herself out as being an immigration specialist, immigration consultant or any other title or description reflecting an expertise in immigration matters shall advertise in any manner whatsoever that he or she is a notary public.

(b) A notary public qualified and bonded as an immigration consultant under chapter 19.5 (commencing with Section 22440) of Division 8 of the Business and Professions Code may enter data, provided by the client, on immigration forms provided by a federal or state agency. The fee for this service shall not exceed ten dollars ($10) per individual for each set of forms. If notary services are performed in relation to the set of immigration forms, additional fees may be collected pursuant to Section 8211. This fee limitation shall not apply to an attorney, who is also a notary public, who is rendering professional services regarding immigration matters.

(c) Nothing in this section shall be construed to exempt a notary public who enters data on an immigration form at the direction of a client, or otherwise performs the services of an immigration consultant, as defined by Section 22441 of the Business and Professions Code, from the requirements of Chapter 19.5 (commencing with Section 22440) of Division 8 of the Business and Professions Code. A notary public who is not qualified and bonded as an immigration consultant under Chapter 19.5 (commencing with section 22440) of Division 8 of the Business and Professions Code may not enter data provided by a client on immigration forms nor otherwise perform the services of an immigration consultant.

§ 8224. A notary public who has a direct financial or beneficial interest in a transaction shall not perform any notarial act in connection with such transaction.

For purposes of this section, a notary public has a direct financial or beneficial interest in a transaction if the notary public:

(a) With respect to a financial transaction, is named, individually, as a principal to the transaction.

(b) With respect to real property, is named, individually, as a grantor, grantee, mortgagor, mortgagee, trustor, trustee, beneficiary, vendor, vendee, lessor, or lessee, to the transaction.

For purposes of this section, a notary public has no direct financial or beneficial interest in a transaction where the notary public acts in the capacity of an agent, employee, insurer, attorney, escrow, or lender for a person having a direct financial or beneficial interest in the transaction.

§ 8224.1. A notary public shall not take the acknowledgment or proof of instruments of writing executed by the notary public nor shall depositions or affidavits of the notary public be taken by the notary public.

§ 8225. (a) Any person who solicits, coerces, or in any manner influences a notary public to perform an improper notarial act knowing that act to be an improper notarial act, including any act required of a notary public under Section 8206, shall be guilty of a misdemeanor.

(b) Notwithstanding any other limitation of time described in Section 802 of the Penal Code, or any other provision of law, prosecution for a violation of this offense shall be commenced within four years after discovery of the commission of the offense, or within four years after the completion of the offense, whichever is later.

(c) The penalty provided by this section is not an exclusive remedy, and does not affect any other relief or remedy provided by law.

§ 8227.1. It shall be a misdemeanor for any person who is not a duly commissioned, qualified, and acting notary public for the State of California to do any of the following:

(a) Represent or hold himself or herself out to the public or to any person as being entitled to act as a notary public.

(b) Assume, use or advertise the title of notary public in such a manner as to convey the impression that the person is a notary public.

(c) Purport to act as a notary public.

§ 8227.3. Any person who is not a duly commissioned, qualified, and acting notary public who does any of the acts prohibited by Section 8227.1 in relation to any document or instrument affecting title to, placing an encumbrance on, or placing an interest secured by a mortgage or deed of trust on, real property consisting of a single-family residence containing not more than four dwelling units, is guilty of a felony.

§ 8228. The Secretary of State or a peace officer, as defined in Sections 830.1, 830.2, and 830.3 of the Penal Code, possessing reasonable suspicion and acting in his or her official capacity and within his or her authority, may enforce the provisions of this chapter through the examination of a notary public's books, records, letters, contracts, and other pertinent documents relating to the official acts of the notary public.

§ 8228.1. (a) Any notary public who willfully fails to perform any duty required of a notary public under Section 8206, or who willfully fails to keep the seal of the notary public under the direct and exclusive control of the notary public, or who surrenders the seal of the notary public to any person not otherwise authorized by law to possess the seal of the notary, shall be guilty of a misdemeanor.

(b) Notwithstanding any other limitation of time described in Section 802 of the Penal Code or any other provision of law, prosecution for a violation of this offense shall be commenced within four years after discovery of the commission of the offense, or within four years after the completion of the offense, whichever is later.

(c) The penalty provided by this section is not an exclusive remedy, and does not affect any other relief or remedy provided by law.

§ 8230. If a notary public executes a jurat and the statement sworn or subscribed to is contained in a document purporting to identify the affiant, and includes the birth date or age of the person and a purported photograph or finger or thumbprint of the person so swearing or subscribing, the notary public shall require, as a condition to executing the jurat, that the person verify the birth date or age contained in the statement by showing either:

(a) A certified copy of the person's birth certificate, or

(b) An identification card or driver's license issued by the Department of Motor Vehicles.

For the purposes of preparing for submission of forms required by the United States Immigration and Naturalization Service, and only for such purposes, a notary public may also accept for identification any documents or declarations acceptable to the United States Immigration and Naturalization Service.

§ 27201.5. (a) A notary acknowledgment shall be deemed complete for recording purposes without a photographically reproducible official seal of the notary public if the seal, as described in Section 8207, is present and legible, and the name of the notary, the county of the notary's principal place of business, the notary's telephone number, the notary's registration number, and the notary's commission expiration date are typed or printed in a manner that is photographically reproducible below, or immediately adjacent to, the notary's signature in the acknowledgment.

(b) If a request for a certified copy of a birth or death record is received by mail, a notarized statement sworn under penalty of perjury shall accompany the request, stating that the requester is an authorized person, as defined by law.

§ 27287. Unless it belongs to the class provided for in either Sections 27282 to 27286, inclusive, or Sections 1202 or 1203, of the Civil Code, or is a fictitious mortgage or deed of trust as provided in Sections 2952, or 2963, of the Civil Code, or is a fictitious oil and gas lease as provided in Section 1219 of the Civil Code, or is a claim of lien, as provided in Section 3084 of the Civil Code, or a notice of completion, as provided in Section 3093 of the Civil Code, before an instrument can be recorded its execution shall be acknowledged by the person executing it, or if executed by a corporation, by its president or secretary or other person executing it on behalf of the corporation, or, except for any quitclaim deed grant deed mortgage, deed of trust, or security agreement or other deed of trust affecting real property, proved by subscribing witness or as provided in Sections 1198 and 1199 of the Civil Code, and the acknowledgment or proof certified as prescribed by law. This section shall not apply to a trustee's deed resulting from a decree of foreclosure, or a nonjudicial foreclosure pursuant to Section 2924 of the Civil Code, or to a deed of reconveyance.

§ 27361. (a) The fee for recording and indexing every instrument, paper, or notice required or permitted by law to be recorded shall not exceed ten dollars ($10) for recording the first page and three dollars ($3) for each additional page, except the recorder may charge additional fees as follows:

(1) If the printing on printed forms is spaced more than nine lines per vertical inch or more than 22 characters and spaces per inch measured horizontally for not less than 3 inches in one sentence, the recorder shall charge one dollar ($1) extra for each page or sheet on which printing appears excepting, however, the extra charge shall not apply to printed words which are directive or explanatory in nature for completion of the form or on vital statistics forms. Fees collected under this paragraph are not subject to subdivision (b) or (c).

(2) If a page or sheet does not conform with the dimensions described in subdivision (a) of Section 27361.5, the recorder shall charge three dollars ($3) extra per page or sheet of the document. The extra charge authorized under this paragraph shall be available solely to support, maintain, improve, and provide for the full operation for modernized creation, retention, and retrieval of information in each county's system of recorded documents.***

§ 27361.5. (a) As used in Section 27361, a page shall be one printed side of a single piece of paper being 8½ inches by 11 inches.

(b) A sheet shall be one printed side of a single piece of paper which is not exactly 8½ inches by 11 inches but not greater than 8½ inches by 14 inches.

§ 27361.7. Whenever the text of a document presented for record may be made out but is not sufficiently legible to reproduce a readable photographic record, the recorder may require the person presenting it for record to substitute a legible original document or to prepare a legible copy of the first document by handwriting or typewriting and attach the same to the original as a part of the document for making the permanent photographic record. The handwritten or typewritten legible copy shall be certified by the party creating the copy under penalty of perjury as being a true copy of the original. As used in this section, the word "text" includes the notary seal, certificates, and other appendages thereto.

§ 27391. (a) Upon approval by resolution of the board of supervisors and system certification by the Attorney General, a county recorder may establish an electronic recording delivery system. ***

(e) When a signature is required to be accompanied by a notary's seal or stamp, that requirement is satisfied if the electronic signature of the notary contains all of the following:

(1) The name of the notary.

(2) The words "Notary Public."

(3) The name of the county where the bond and oath of office of the notary are filed.

(4) The sequential identification number assigned to the notary, if any.

(5) The sequential identification number assigned to the manufacturer or vendor of the notary's physical or electronic seal, if any.

§ 66436. (a) A statement, signed and acknowledged by all parties having any record title interest in the subdivided real property, consenting to the preparation and recordation of the final map is required, ***

(c) A notary acknowledgment shall be deemed complete for recording without the official seal of the notary, so long as the name of the notary, the county of the notary's principal place of business, and the notary's commission expiration date are typed or printed below or immediately adjacent to the notary's signature in the acknowledgment.

Business and Professions Code

§ 6125. No person shall practice law in California unless the person is an active member of the State Bar.

§ 6126. (a) Any person advertising or holding himself or herself out as practicing or entitled to practice law or otherwise practicing law who is not an active member of the State Bar, is guilty of a misdemeanor. ***

§ 6126.7 (a) It is a violation of subdivision (a) of Section 6126 for any person who is not an attorney to literally translate from English into another language, in any document, including an advertisement, stationery, letterhead, business card, or other comparable written material, any words or titles, including, but not limited to, "notary public," "notary," "licensed," "attorney," or "lawyer," that imply that the person is an attorney. As provided in this subdivision, the literal translation of the phrase "notary public" into Spanish as "notario publico" or "notario," is expressly prohibited.

(b) For purposes of this section, "literal translation of" or "to literally translate" a word, title, or phrase from one language means the translation of a word, title, or phrase without regard to the true meaning of the word or phrase in the language that is being translated.

(c) (1) In addition to any other remedies and penalties prescribed in this article, a person who violates this section shall be subject to a civil penalty not to exceed one thousand dollars ($1,000) per day for each violation, to be assessed and collected in a civil action brought by the State Bar.

(2) In assessing the amount of the civil penalty, the court may consider relevant circumstances presented by the parties to the case, including, but not limited to, the following:

(A) The nature and severity of the misconduct.

(B) The number of violations.

(C) The length of time over which the misconduct occurred, and the persistence of the misconduct.

(D) The willfulness of the misconduct.

(E) The defendant's assets, liabilities, and net worth.

(3) The court shall grant a prevailing plaintiff reasonable attorneys' fees and costs.

(4) A civil action brought under this section shall be commenced within four years after the cause of action accrues.

(5) In a civil action brought by the State Bar under this section, the civil penalty collected shall be paid to the State Bar and allocated to the fund established pursuant to Section 6033 to provide free legal services related to immigration reform act services to clients of limited means or to a fund for the purposes of mitigating unpaid claims of injured immigrant clients under Section 22447, as directed by the Board of Trustees of the State Bar. The board shall annually report any collection and expenditure of funds for the preceding calendar year, as authorized by this section, to the Assembly and Senate Committees on Judiciary. The report required by this section may be included in the report described in Section 6086.15.

§ 6127. The following acts or omissions in respect to the practice of law are contempts of the authority of the courts:

(a) Assuming to be an officer or attorney of a court and acting as such, without authority.

(b) Advertising or holding oneself out as practicing or as entitled to practice law or otherwise practicing law in any court, without being an active member of the State Bar.

Proceedings to adjudge a person in contempt of court under this section are to be taken in accordance with the provisions of Title V of Part III of the Code of Civil Procedure.

§ 22442.2. (a) An immigration consultant shall conspicuously display in his or her office a notice that shall be at least 12 inches by 20 inches with boldface type or print with each character at least one inch in height and width in English and in the native language of the consultant's clientele, the following information:

(1) The full name, address, and evidence of compliance with any applicable bonding requirement including the bond number, if any.

(2) A statement that the consultant is not an attorney.

(b) Prior to providing any services, an immigration consultant shall provide the client with written disclosure which shall include the immigration consultant's name, address, telephone number, agent for service of process, and evidence of compliance with any applicable bonding requirement, including the bond number, if any.

§ 22442.3. (a) An immigration consultant shall not, with the intent to mislead, literally translate, from English into another language, any words or titles, including, but not limited to, "notary public," "notary," "licensed," "attorney," or lawyer, that imply that the person is an attorney, in any document, including an advertisement, stationery, letterhead, business card, or other comparable written material describing the immigration consultant. As provided in this subdivision, the literal translation of phrase "notary public" into Spanish as "notario public" or "notaria" is expressly prohibited.

(b) For purposes of this section, "literal translation of" or "to literally translate" a word, title or phrase from one language means the translation of a word or phrase without regard to the true meaning of the word or phrase in the language that is being translated.

(c) An immigration consultant may not make or authorize the making of any verbal or written references to his or her compliance with the bonding requirements of Section 22443.1 except as provided in this chapter.

(d) A violation of subdivision (a) or (c) by an immigration consultant shall constitute a violation of subdivision (a) of Section 6126.

(e) (1) In addition to the remedies and penalties prescribed in this chapter, a person who violates this section shall be subject to a civil penalty not to exceed one thousand dollars ($1,000) per day for each violation, to be assessed and collected in a civil action brought by any person injured by the violation or in a civil action brought in the name of the people of the State of California by the Attorney General, a district attorney, or a city attorney.

(2) In assessing the amount of the civil penalty, the court may consider relevant circumstances presented by the parties to the case, including, but not limited to, the following:

(A) The nature and severity of the misconduct.

(B) The number of violations.

(C) The length of time over which the misconduct occurred, and the persistence of the misconduct.

(D) The willfulness of the misconduct.

(E) The defendant's assets, liabilities, and net worth.

(3) If the Attorney General brings the action, one-half of the civil penalty collected shall be paid to the treasurer of the county in which the judgment was entered, and one-half to the General Fund. If a district attorney brings the action, the civil penalty collected shall be paid to the treasurer of the county in which the judgment was entered. If a city attorney brings the action, one-half of the civil penalty collected shall be paid to the treasurer of the city in which the judgment was entered, and one-half to the treasurer of the county in which the judgment was entered.

(4) The court shall grant a prevailing plaintiff reasonable attorneys' fees and costs.

Civil Code

§ 14. Words used in this code in the present tense include the future as well as the present; words used in the masculine gender include the feminine and neuter; the singular number includes the plural, and the plural the singular; the word person includes a corporation as well as a natural person; county includes city and county; writing includes printing and typewriting; oath includes affirmation or declaration; and every mode of oral statement, under oath or affirmation, is embraced by the term "testify," and every written one in the term "depose"; signature or subscription includes mark, when the person cannot write, his name being written near it, by a person who writes his own name as a witness; provided, that when a signature is by mark it must in order that the same may be acknowledged or may serve as the signature to any sworn statement be witnessed by two persons who must subscribe their own names as witnesses thereto. ***

§ 1181. The proof or acknowledgment of an instrument may be made before a notary public at any place within this state, or within the county or city and

CALIFORNIA NOTARY LAW PRIMER

county in this state in which the officer specified below was elected or appointed, before either:
  (a) A clerk of a superior, municipal, or justice court.
  (b) A county clerk.
  (c) A court commissioner.
  (d) A judge or retired judge of a municipal or justice court.
  (e) A district attorney.
  (f) A clerk of a board of supervisors.
  (g) A city clerk.
  (h) A county counsel.
  (i) A city attorney.
  (j) Secretary of the Senate.
  (k) Chief Clerk of the Assembly.

§ 1182. The proof or acknowledgment of an instrument may be made without this state, but within the United States, and within the jurisdiction of the officer, before any of the following:
  (1) A justice, judge, or clerk of any court of record of the United States.
  (2) A justice, judge, or clerk of any court of record of any state.
  (3) A commissioner appointed by the Governor or Secretary of State for that purpose.
  (4) A notary public.
  (5) Any other officer of the state where the acknowledgment is made authorized by its laws to take such proof or acknowledgment.

§ 1183. The proof or acknowledgment of an instrument may be made without the United States, before any of the following:
  (a) A minister, commissioner, or charge d'affaires of the United States, resident and accredited in the country where the proof or acknowledgment is made.
  (b) A consul, vice consul, or consular agent of the United States, resident in the country where the proof or acknowledgment is made.
  (c) A judge of a court of record of the country where the proof or acknowledgment is made.
  (d) Commissioners appointed by the Governor or Secretary of State for that purpose.
  (e) A notary public.

If the proof or acknowledgment is made before a notary public, the signature of the notary public shall be proved or acknowledged (1) before a judge of a court of record of the country where the proof or acknowledgment is made, or (2) by any American diplomatic officer, consul general, consul, vice consul, or consular agent, or (3) by an apostille (certification) affixed to the instrument pursuant to the terms of The Hague Convention Abolishing the Requirement of Legalization for Foreign Public Documents.

§ 1183.5. Any officer on active duty or performing inactive-duty training in the armed forces having the general powers of a notary public pursuant to Section 936 or 1044a of Title 10 of the United States Code (Public Law 90-632 and 101-510) and any successor statutes may perform all notarial acts for any person serving in the armed forces of the United States, wherever he or she may be, or for any spouse of a person serving in the armed forces, wherever he or she may be, or for any person eligible for legal assistance under laws and regulations of the United States, wherever he or she may be, for any person serving with, employed by, or accompanying such armed forces outside the United States and outside the Canal Zone, Puerto Rico, Guam and the Virgin Islands, and any person subject to the Uniform Code of Military Justice outside of the United States.

Any instrument acknowledged by any such officer or any oath or affirmation made before such officer shall not be rendered invalid by the failure to state therein the place of execution or acknowledgment. No seal or authentication of the officer's certificate of acknowledgment or of any jurat signed by him or her shall be required but the officer taking the acknowledgment shall endorse thereon or attach thereto a certificate substantially in a form authorized by the laws of this state or in the following form:

On this the ____ day of ____, 20__, before me _____, the undersigned officer, personally appeared _____ known to me (or satisfactorily proven) to be (a) serving in the armed forces of the United States, (b) a spouse of a person serving in the armed forces of the United States, or (c) a person serving with, employed by, or accompanying the armed forces of the United States outside the United States and outside the Canal Zone, Puerto Rico, Guam, and the Virgin Islands, and to be the person whose name is subscribed to the within instrument and acknowledged that he or she executed the same. And the undersigned does further certify that he or she is at the date of this certificate a commissioned officer of the armed forces of the United States having the general powers of a notary public under the provisions of Section 936 or 1044a of Title 10 of the United States Code (Public Law 90-632 and 101-510).

_____ Signature of officer,
_____ rank, branch of service and capacity in which signed.

To any affidavit subscribed and sworn to before such officer there shall be attached a jurat substantially in the following form:

Subscribed and sworn to before me on this ____ day of _____, 19__. _____ Signature of officer, _____ rank, branch of service and capacity in which signed.

The recitals contained in any such certificate or jurat shall be prima facie evidence of the truth thereof, and any certificate of acknowledgment, oath or affirmation purporting to have been made by any commissioned officer of the Army, Air Force, Navy, Marine Corps or Coast Guard shall, notwithstanding the omission of any specific recitals therein, constitute presumptive evidence of the existence of the facts necessary to authorize such acknowledgment, oath or affirmation to be taken by the certifying officer pursuant to this section.

§ 1185. (a) The acknowledgment of an instrument shall not be taken unless the officer taking it has satisfactory evidence that the person making the acknowledgment is the individual who is described in and who executed the instrument.

(b) For purposes of this section "satisfactory evidence" means the absence of information, evidence, or other circumstances that would lead a reasonable person to believe that the person making the acknowledgment is not the individual he or she claims to be and any one of the following:

(1) (A) The oath or affirmation of a credible witness personally known to the officer, whose identity is proven to the officer upon presentation of a document satisfying the requirements of paragraph (3) or (4), that the person making the acknowledgment is personally known to the witness and that each of the following are true:

(i) The person making the acknowledgment is the person named in the document.

(ii) The person making the acknowledgment is personally known to the witness.

(iii) That it is the reasonable belief of the witness that the circumstances of the person making the acknowledgment are such that it would be very difficult or impossible for that person to obtain another form of identification.

(iv) The person making the acknowledgment does not possess any of the identification documents named in paragraphs (3) and (4).

(v) The witness does not have a financial interest in the document being acknowledged and is not named in the document.

(B) A notary public who violates this section by failing to obtain the satisfactory evidence required by subparagraph (A) shall be subject to a civil penalty not exceeding ten thousand dollars ($10,000). An action to impose this civil penalty may be brought by the Secretary of State in an administrative proceeding or a public prosecutor in superior court, and shall be enforced as a civil judgment. A public prosecutor shall inform the secretary of any civil penalty imposed under this subparagraph.

(2) The oath or affirmation under penalty of perjury of two credible witnesses, whose identities are proven to the officer upon the presentation of a document satisfying the requirements of paragraph (3) or (4), that each statement in paragraph (1) is true.

(3) Reasonable reliance on the presentation to the officer of any one of the following, if the document is current or has been issued within five years:

(A) An identification card or driver's license issued by the Department of Motor Vehicles.

(B) A passport issued by the Department of State of the United States.

(C) An inmate identification card issued by the Department of Corrections and Rehabilitation, if the inmate is in custody in prison.

(4) Reasonable reliance on the presentation of any one of the following, provided that a document specified in subparagraphs (A) to (F), inclusive, shall either be current or have been issued within five years and shall contain a photograph and description of the person named on it, shall be signed by the person, shall bear a serial or other identifying number, and, in the event that the document is a passport, shall have been stamped by the United States Citizenship and Immigration Services of the Department of Homeland Security:

(A) A passport issued by a foreign government.

(B) A driver's license issued by a state other than California or by a Canadian or Mexican public agency authorized to issue driver's licenses.

(C) An identification card issued by a state other than California.

(D) An identification card issued by any branch of the Armed Forces of the United States.

(E) An employee identification card issued by an agency or office of the State of California, or by an agency or office of a city, county, or city and county in this state.

(c) An officer who has taken an acknowledgment pursuant to this section shall be presumed to have operated in accordance with the provisions of law.

(d) A party who files an action for damages based on the failure of the officer to establish the proper identity of the person making the acknowledgment shall have the burden of proof in establishing the negligence or misconduct of the officer.

(e) A person convicted of perjury under this section shall forfeit any financial interest in the document.

§ 1188. An officer taking the acknowledgment of an instrument shall endorse thereon or attach thereto a certificate pursuant to Section 1189.

§ 1189. (a) (1) Any certificate of acknowledgment taken within this state shall include a notice at the top of the certificate of acknowledgment in an enclosed box stating: "A notary public or other officer completing this certificate verifies only the identity of the individual who signed the document to which this certificate is attached, and not the truthfulness, accuracy, or validity of that document." This notice shall be legible.

(2) The physical format of the boxed notice at the top of the certificate of acknowledgment required pursuant to paragraph (3) is an example, for purposes of illustration and not limitation, of the physical format of a boxed notice fulfilling the requirements of paragraph (1).

(3) A certificate of acknowledgment taken within this state shall be in the following form:

> A notary public or other officer completing this certificate verifies only the identity of the individual who signed the document to which this certificate is attached, and not the truthfulness, accuracy, or validity of that document.

State of California   )
County of _____)

On _____ before me, (here insert name and title of the officer), personally appeared _____, who proved to me on the basis of satisfactory evidence to be the person(s) whose name(s) is/are subscribed to the within instrument and acknowledged to me that he/she/they executed the same in his/her/their authorized capacity(ies), and that by his/her/their signature(s) on the instrument the person(s), or the entity upon behalf of which the person(s) acted, executed the instrument.

I certify under PENALTY OF PERJURY under the laws of the State of California that the foregoing paragraph is true and correct.

WITNESS my hand and official seal.

Signature   (Seal)

(4) A notary public who willfully states as true any material fact that he or she knows to be false shall be subject to a civil penalty not exceeding ten thousand dollars ($10,000). An action to impose a civil penalty under this subdivision may be brought by the Secretary of State in an administrative proceeding or any public prosecutor in superior court, and shall be enforced as a civil judgment. A public prosecutor shall inform the secretary of any civil penalty imposed under this section.

(b) Any certificate of acknowledgment taken in another place shall be sufficient in this state if it is taken in accordance with the laws of the place where the acknowledgment is made.

(c) On documents to be filed in another state or jurisdiction of the United States, a California notary public may complete any acknowledgment form as may be required in that other state or jurisdiction on a document, provided the form does not require the notary to determine or certify that the signer holds a particular representative capacity or to make other determinations and certifications not allowed by California law.

(d) An acknowledgment provided prior to January 1, 1993, and conforming to applicable provisions of former Sections 1189, 1190, 1190a, 1190.1, 1191, and 1192, as repealed by Chapter 335 of the Statutes of 1990, shall have the same force and effect as if those sections had not been repealed.

§ 1190. The certificate of acknowledgment of an instrument executed on behalf of an incorporated or unincorporated entity by a duly authorized person in the form specified in Section 1189 shall be prima facie evidence that the instrument is the duly authorized act of the entity named in the instrument and shall be conclusive evidence thereof in favor of any good faith purchaser, lessee, or encumbrancer. "Duly authorized person," with respect to a domestic or foreign corporation, includes the president, vice president, secretary, and assistant secretary of the corporation.

§ 1193. Officers taking and certifying acknowledgments or proof of instruments for record, must authenticate their certificates by affixing thereto their signatures, followed by the names of their offices; also, their seals of office, if by the laws of the State or country where the acknowledgment or proof is taken, or by authority of which they are acting, they are required to have official seals.

§ 1195. (a) Proof of the execution of an instrument, when not acknowledged, may be made by any of the following:

(1) By the party executing it, or either of them.
(2) By a subscribing witness.
(3) By other witnesses, in cases mentioned in Section 1198.

(b) (1) Proof of the execution of a power of attorney, grant deed, mortgage, deed of trust, quitclaim deed, security agreement, or any instrument affecting real property is not permitted pursuant to Section 27287 of the Government Code, though proof of the execution of a trustee's deed or deed of reconveyance is permitted.

(2) Proof of the execution for any instrument requiring a notary public to obtain a thumbprint from the party signing the document in the notary public's journal is not permitted.

(c) Any certificate for proof of execution taken within this state shall include a notice at the top of the certificate for proof of execution in an enclosed box stating: "A notary public or other officer completing this certificate verifies only the identity of the individual who signed the document to which this certificate is attached, and not the truthfulness, accuracy, or validity of that document." This notice shall be legible.

(d) The physical format of the boxed notice at the top of the certificate for proof of execution required pursuant to subdivision (e) is an example, for purposes of illustration and not limitation, of the physical format of a boxed notice fulfilling the requirements of subdivision (c).

(e) A certificate for proof of execution taken within this state shall be in the following form:

> A notary public or other officer completing this certificate verifies only the identity of the individual who signed the document to which this certificate is attached, and not the truthfulness, accuracy, or validity of that document.

State of California) ss.
County of _____)

On _____ (date), before me, _____ (name and title of officer), personally appeared _____ (name of subscribing witness), proved to me to be the person whose name is subscribed to the within instrument, as a witness thereto, on the oath of _____ (name of credible witness), a credible witness who is known to me and provided a satisfactory identifying document. _____ (name of subscribing witness), being by me duly sworn, said that he/she was present and saw/heard _____ (name[s] of principal[s]), the same person(s) described in and whose name(s) is/are subscribed to the within or attached instrument in his/her/their authorized capacity(ies) as (a) party(ies) thereto, execute or acknowledge executing the same, and that said affiant subscribed his/her name to the within or attached instrument as a witness at the request of _____ (name[s] of principal[s]).

WITNESS my hand and official seal.

Signature   (Seal)

§ 1196. A witness shall be proved to be a subscribing witness by the oath of a credible witness who provides the officer with any document satisfying the requirements of paragraph (3) or (4) of subdivision (b) of Section 1185.

§ 1197. The subscribing witness must prove that the person whose name is subscribed to the instrument as a party is the person described in it, and that such person executed it, and that the witness subscribed his name thereto as a witness.

§ 1363.03. a) An association shall adopt rules, in accordance with the procedures prescribed by Article 4 (commencing with Section 1357.100) of Chapter 2, that do all of the following:

(1) Ensure that if any candidate or member advocating a point of view is provided access to association media, newsletters, or Internet websites during a campaign, for purposes that are reasonably related to that election, equal access shall be provided to all candidates and members advocating a point of view, including those not endorsed by the board, for purposes that are reasonably related to the election. The association shall not edit or redact any content from these communications, but may include a statement specifying that the candidate or member, and not the association, is responsible for that content.

(2) Ensure access to the common area meeting space, if any exists, during a campaign, at no cost, to all candidates, including those who are not incumbents, and to all members advocating a point of view, including those not endorsed by the board, for purposes reasonably related to the election.

(3) Specify the qualifications for candidates for the board of directors and any other elected position, and procedures for the nomination of candidates. A nomination or election procedure shall not be deemed reasonable if it disallows any member of the association from nominating himself or herself for election to the board of directors.

(4) Specify the qualifications for voting, the voting power of each membership, the authenticity, validity, and effect of proxies, and the voting period for elections, including the times at which polls will open and close.

(5) Specify a method of selecting one or three independent third parties as inspector, or inspectors, of election utilizing one of the following methods:

(A) Appointment of the inspector or inspectors by the board.

(B) Election of the inspector or inspectors by the members of the association.

(C) Any other method for selecting the inspector or inspectors.

(b) Notwithstanding any other law or provision of the governing documents, an election within a common interest development regarding assessments, selection of members of the association board of directors, amendments to the governing documents, or the grant of exclusive use of common area property pursuant to Section 1363.07 shall be held by secret ballot in accordance with the procedures set forth in this section.

(c) (1) The association shall select an independent third party or parties as an inspector of election. The number of inspectors of election shall be one or three.

(2) For the purposes of this section, an independent third party includes, but is not limited to, a volunteer poll worker with the county registrar of voters, a licensee of the California Board of Accountancy, or a notary public. An independent third party may be a member of the association, but may not be a member of the board of directors or a candidate for the board of directors or related to a member of the board of directors or a candidate for the board of directors. An independent third party may not be a person who is currently employed or under contract to the association for any compensable services unless expressly authorized by rules of the association adopted pursuant to paragraph (5) of subdivision (a).

(3) The inspector or inspectors of election shall do all of the following:

(A) Determine the number of memberships entitled to vote and the voting power of each.

(B) Determine the authenticity, validity, and effect of proxies, if any.

(C) Receive ballots.

(D) Hear and determine all challenges and questions in any way arising out of or in connection with the right to vote.

(E) Count and tabulate all votes.

(F) Determine when the polls shall close.

(G) Determine the result of the election.

(H) Perform any acts as may be proper to conduct the election with fairness to all members in accordance with this section and all applicable rules of the association regarding the conduct of the election that are not in conflict with this section.

(4) An inspector of election shall perform his or her duties impartially, in good faith, to the best of his or her ability, and as expeditiously as is practical. If there are three inspectors of election, the decision or act of a majority shall be effective in all respects as the decision or act of all. Any report made by the inspector or inspectors of election is prima facie evidence of the facts stated in the report.

(d) Any instruction given in a proxy issued for an election that directs the manner in which the proxy holder is to cast the vote shall be set forth on a separate page of the proxy that can be detached and given to the proxy holder to retain. The proxy holder shall cast the member's vote by secret ballot.

(e) Ballots and two preaddressed envelopes with instructions on how to return ballots shall be mailed by first-class mail or delivered by the association to every member not less than 30 days prior to the deadline for voting. In order to preserve confidentiality, a voter may not be identified by name, address, or lot, parcel, or unit number on the ballot. The association shall use as a model those procedures used by California counties for ensuring confidentiality of voter absentee ballots, including all of the following:

(1) The ballot itself is not signed by the voter, but is inserted into an envelope that is sealed. This envelope is inserted into a second envelope that is sealed. In the upper left hand corner of the second envelope, the voter prints and signs his or her name, address, and lot, or parcel, or unit number that entitles him or her to vote.

(2) The second envelope is addressed to the inspector or inspectors of election, who will be tallying the votes. The envelope may be mailed or delivered by hand to a location specified by the inspector or inspectors of election. The member may request a receipt for delivery.

(f) All votes shall be counted and tabulated by the inspector or inspectors of election in public at a properly noticed open meeting of the board of directors or members. Any candidate or other member of the association may witness the counting and tabulation of the votes. No person, including a member of the association or an employee of the management company, shall open or otherwise review any ballot prior to the time and place at which the ballots are counted and tabulated.

(g) The results of the election shall be promptly reported to the board of directors of the association and shall be recorded in the minutes of the next meeting of the board of directors and shall be available for review by members of the association. Within 15 days of the election, the board shall publicize the results of the election in a communication directed to all members.

(h) The sealed ballots at all times shall be in the custody of the inspector or inspectors of election or at a location designated by the inspector or inspectors until after the tabulation of the vote, at which time custody shall be transferred to the association.

(i) After tabulation, election ballots shall be stored by the association in a secure place for no less than one year after the date of the election. In the event of a recount or other challenge to the election process, the association shall, upon written request, make the ballots available for inspection and review by association members or their authorized representatives. Any recount shall be conducted in a manner that shall preserve the confidentiality of the vote.

(j) The provisions of this section apply to both incorporated and unincorporated associations, notwithstanding any contrary provision of the governing documents.

§ 1633.1. This title may be cited as the Uniform Electronic Transaction Act.***

§ 1633.11. (a) If a law requires that a signature be notarized, the requirement is satisfied with respect to an electronic signature if an electronic record includes, in addition to the electronic signature to be notarized, the electronic signature of a notary public together with all other information required to be included in a notarization by other applicable law.

(b) In a transaction, if a law requires that a statement be signed under penalty of perjury, the requirement is satisfied with respect to an electronic signature, if an electronic record includes, in addition to the electronic signature, all of the information as to which the declaration pertains together with a declaration under penalty of perjury by the person who submits the electronic signature that the information is true and correct.

§ 1633.12. (a) If the law requires that a record be retained, the requirement is satisfied by retaining an electronic record of the information in the record, if the electronic record reflects accurately the information set forth in the record at the time it was first generated in its final form as an electronic record or otherwise, and the electronic record remains accessible for later reference. ***

Code of Civil Procedure

§ 335. The periods prescribed for the commencement of actions other than for the recovery of real property, are as follows:

§ 338. Within three years: ***

(f) (1) An action against a notary public on his or her bond or in his or her official capacity except that any cause of action based on malfeasance or misfeasance is not deemed to have accrued until discovery, by the aggrieved party or his or her agent, of the facts constituting the cause of action.

(2) Notwithstanding paragraph (1), an action based on malfeasance or misfeasance shall be commenced within one year from discovery, by the aggrieved party or his or her agent, of the facts constituting the cause of action or within

three years from the performance of the notarial act giving rise to the action, whichever is later.

(3) Notwithstanding paragraph (1), an action against a notary public on his or her bond or in his or her official capacity shall be commenced within six years. ***

§ 1935. A subscribing witness is one who sees a writing executed or hears it acknowledged, and at the request of the party thereupon signs his name as a witness.

§ 2025. ***

(k) Except as provided in paragraph (3) of subdivision (d) of Section 2020, the deposition shall be conducted under the supervision of an officer who is authorized to administer an oath. This officer shall not be financially interested in the action and shall not be a relative or employee of any attorney of any of the parties, or of any of the parties. Any objection to the qualifications of the deposition officer is waived unless made before the deposition begins or as soon thereafter as the ground for that objection becomes known or could be discovered by reasonable diligence.

(l) (1) The deposition officer shall put the deponent under oath. Unless the parties agree or the court orders otherwise, the testimony, as well as any stated objections, shall be taken stenographically. The party noticing the deposition may also record the testimony by audiotape or videotape if the notice of deposition stated an intention also to record the testimony by either of those methods, or if all the parties agree that the testimony may also be recorded by either of those methods. Any other party, at that party's expense, may make a simultaneous audiotape or videotape record of the deposition, provided that other party promptly, and in no event less than three calendar days before the date for which the deposition is scheduled, serves a written notice of this intention to audiotape or videotape the deposition testimony on the party or attorney who noticed the deposition, on all other parties or attorneys on whom the deposition notice was served under subdivision (c), and on any deponent whose attendance is being compelled by a deposition subpoena under Section 2020. If this notice is given three calendar days before the deposition date, it shall be made by personal service under Section 1011. Examination and cross-examination of the deponent shall proceed as permitted at trial under the provisions of the Evidence Code. ***

§ 2026. ***

(c) A deposition taken under this section shall be conducted (1) under the supervision of a person who is authorized to administer oaths by the laws of the United States or those of the place where the examination is to be held, and who is not otherwise disqualified under subdivision (k) of Section 2025, or (2) before a person appointed by the court. This appointment is effective to authorize that person to administer oaths and to take testimony. When necessary or convenient, the court shall issue a commission on such terms and with such directions as are just and appropriate. ***

§ 2027. ***

(c) A deposition taken under this section shall be conducted (1) under the supervision of a person who is authorized to administer oaths or their equivalent by the laws of the United States or of the foreign nation, and who is not otherwise disqualified under subdivision (k) of Section 2025, or (2) a person or officer appointed by commission or under letters rogatory; or (3) any person agreed to by all the parties. ***

§ 2093. (a) Every court, every judge, or clerk of any court, every justice, and every notary public, and every officer or person authorized to take testimony in any action or proceeding, or to decide upon evidence, has the power to administer oaths or affirmations.

(b) Every shorthand reporter certified pursuant to Article 3 (commencing with Section 8020) of Chapter 13 of Division 3 of the Business and Professions Code has the power to administer oaths or affirmations and may perform the duties of the deposition officer pursuant to Section 2025. The certified shorthand reporter shall be entitled to receive fees for services rendered during a deposition, including fees for deposition services, as specified in subdivision (c) of Section 8211 of the Government Code.

(c) A former judge or justice of a court of record in this state who retired or resigned from office, other than a judge or justice who was retired by the Supreme Court for disability, shall have the power to administer oaths or affirmations, if the former judge or justice requests and receives a certification from the Commission on Judicial Performance that there was no formal disciplinary proceeding pending at the time of retirement or resignation. Where no formal disciplinary proceeding was pending at the time of retirement or resignation, the Commission on Judicial Performance shall issue the certification.

No law, rule, or regulation regarding the confidentiality of proceedings of the Commission on Judicial Performance shall be construed to prohibit the Commission on Judicial Performance from issuing a certificate as provided for in this section.

§ 2094. An oath, or affirmation, in an action or proceeding, may be administered as follows, the person who swears, or affirms, expressing his assent when addressed in the following form: "You do solemnly swear (or affirm, as the case may be), that the evidence you shall give in this issue (or matter), pending between ____ and ____, shall be the truth, the whole truth, and nothing but the truth, so help you God."

Elections Code

§ 8080. No fee or charge shall be made or collected by any officer for verifying any nomination document or circulator's affidavit.

Family Code

§ 503. The county clerk shall issue a confidential marriage license upon the request of a notary public approved by the county clerk to authorize confidential marriages pursuant to Chapter 2 (commencing with Section 530) and upon payment by the notary public of the fees specified in Sections 26840.1 and 26840.8 of the Government Code. The parties shall reimburse a notary public who authorizes a confidential marriage for the amount of the fees.

§ 530. (a) No notary public shall authorize a confidential marriage pursuant to this part unless the notary public is approved by the county clerk to authorize confidential marriages pursuant to this chapter.

(b) A violation of subdivision (a) is a misdemeanor punishable by a fine not to exceed one thousand dollars ($1,000) or six months in jail.

§ 531. (a) An application for approval to authorize confidential marriages pursuant to this part shall be submitted to the county clerk in the county in which the notary public who is applying for the approval resides. The county clerk shall exercise reasonable discretion as to whether to approve applications.

(b) The application shall include all of the following:

(1) The full name of the applicant.

(2) The date of birth of the applicant.

(3) The applicant's current residential address and telephone number.

(4) The address and telephone number of the place where the applicant will issue authorizations for the performance of a marriage.

(5) The full name of the applicant's employer if the applicant is employed by another person.

(6) Whether or not the applicant has engaged in any of the acts specified in Section 8214.1 of the Government Code.

(c) The application shall be accompanied by the fee provided for in Section 536.

§ 532. No approval shall be granted pursuant to this chapter unless the notary public shows evidence of successful completion of a course of instruction concerning the authorization of confidential marriages that shall be conducted by the county clerk. The course of instruction shall not exceed two hours.

§ 533. An approval to authorize confidential marriages pursuant to this chapter is valid for one year. The approval may be renewed for additional one-year periods upon payment of the renewal fee provided for in Section 536.

§ 534. (a) The county clerk shall maintain a list of the notaries public who are approved to authorize confidential marriages. The list shall be available for inspection by the public.

(b) It is the responsibility of a notary public approved to authorize confidential marriages pursuant to this chapter to keep current the information required in paragraphs (1), (3), (4), and (5) of subdivision (b) of Section 531. This information shall be used by the county clerk to update the list required to be maintained by this section.

§ 535. (a) If, after an approval to authorize confidential marriages is granted pursuant to this chapter, it is discovered that the notary public has engaged in any of the actions specified in Section 8214.1 of the Government Code, the approval shall be revoked, and any fees paid by the notary public may be retained by the county clerk.

(b) If a notary public who is approved to authorize confidential marriages pursuant to this chapter is alleged to have violated a provision of this division, the county clerk shall conduct a hearing to determine if the approval of the notary public should be suspended or revoked. The notary public may present such evidence as is necessary in the notary public's defense. If the county clerk determines that the notary public has violated a provision of this division, the county clerk may place the notary public on probation or suspend or revoke the notary public's registration, and any fees paid by the notary public may be retained by the county clerk. The county clerk shall report the findings of the hearing to the Secretary of State for whatever action the Secretary of State deems appropriate.

§ 536. (a) The fee for an application for approval to authorize confidential marriages pursuant to this chapter is three hundred dollars ($300).

(b) The fee for renewal of an approval is three hundred dollars ($300).

(c) Fees received pursuant to this chapter shall be deposited in a trust fund established by the county clerk. The money in the trust fund shall be used exclusively for the administration of the programs described in this chapter.

Penal Code

§ 17. (a) A felony is a crime which is punishable with death or by imprisonment in the state prison. Every other crime or public offense is a misdemeanor except those offenses that are classified as infractions. ***

§ 115. (a) Every person who knowingly procures or offers any false or forged instrument to be filed, registered, or recorded in any public office within this state, which instrument, if genuine, might be filed, registered, or recorded under any law of this state or of the United States, is guilty of a felony. ***

§ 115.5. (a) Every person who files any false or forged document or instrument with the county recorder which affects title to, places an encumbrance on, or places an interest secured by a mortgage or deed of trust on, real property consisting of a single-family residence containing not more than four dwelling units, with knowledge that the document is false or forged, is punishable, in addition to any other punishment, by a fine not exceeding seventy-five thousand dollars ($75,000).

(b) Every person who makes a false sworn statement to a notary public, with knowledge that the statement is false, to induce the notary public to perform an improper notarial act on an instrument or document affecting title to, or placing an encumbrance on, real property consisting of a single-family residence containing not more than four dwelling units is guilty of a felony.

§ 118. (a) Every person who, having taken an oath that he or she will testify, declare, depose, or certify truly before any competent tribunal, officer, or person, in any of the cases in which the oath may by law of the State of California be administered, willfully and contrary to the oath, states as true any material matter which he or she knows to be false, and every person who testifies, declares, deposes, or certifies under penalty of perjury in any of the cases in which the testimony, declarations, depositions, or certification is permitted by law of the State of California under penalty of perjury and willfully states as true any material matter which he or she knows to be false, is guilty of perjury.

This subdivision is applicable whether the statement, or the testimony, declaration, deposition, or certification is made or subscribed within or without the State of California.

(b) No person shall be convicted of perjury where proof of falsity rests solely upon contradiction by testimony of a single person other than the defendant. Proof of falsity may be established by direct or indirect evidence.

§ 126. Perjury is punishable by imprisonment in the state prison for two, three or four years.

§ 470. ***

(b) Every person who, with the intent to defraud, counterfeits or forges the seal or handwriting of another is guilty of forgery.***

(d) Every person who, with the intent to defraud, falsely makes, alters, forges, or counterfeits, utters, publishes, passes or attempts or offers to pass, as true and genuine, any of the following items, knowing the same to be false, altered, forged, or counterfeited, is guilty of forgery: any check, bond, bank bill, or note, cashier's check, traveler's check, money order, post note, draft, any controller's warrant for the payment of money at the treasury, county order or warrant, or request for the payment of money, receipt for money or goods, bill of exchange, promissory note, order, or any assignment of any bond, writing obligatory, or other contract for money or other property, contract, due bill for payment of money or property, receipt for money or property, passage ticket, lottery ticket or share purporting to be issued under the California State Lottery Act of 1984, trading stamp, power of attorney, certificate of ownership or other document evidencing ownership of a vehicle or undocumented vessel, or any certificate of any share, right, or interest in the stock of any corporation or association, or the delivery of goods or chattels of any kind, or for the delivery of any instrument of writing, or acquittance, release or discharge of any debt, account, suit, action, demand, or any other thing, real or personal, or any transfer or assurance of money, certificate of shares of stock, goods, chattels, or other property whatever, or any letter of attorney, or other power to receive money, or to receive or transfer certificates of shares of stock or annuities, or to let, lease, dispose of, alien, or convey any goods, chattels, lands, or tenements, or other estate, real or personal, or falsifies the acknowledgment of any notary public, or any notary public who issues an acknowledgment knowing it to be false; or any matter described in subdivision (b).***

§ 472. Every person who, with intent to defraud another, forges, or counterfeits the seal of this State, the seal of any public officer authorized by law, the seal of any Court of record, or the seal of any corporation, or any other public seal authorized or recognized by the laws of this State, or of any other State, Government, or country, or who falsely makes, forges, or counterfeits any impression purporting to be an impression of any such seal, or who has in his possession any such counterfeited seal or impression thereof, knowing it to be counterfeited, and willfully conceals the same, is guilty of forgery.

§ 473. Forgery is punishable by imprisonment in the state prison, or by imprisonment in the county jail for not more than one year.

§ 653.55. It is a misdemeanor for any person for compensation to knowingly make a false or misleading material statement or assertion of fact in the preparation of an immigration matter which statement or assertion is detrimentally relied upon by another. Such a misdemeanor is punishable by imprisonment in the county jail not exceeding six months, or by a fine not exceeding two thousand five hundred dollars ($2,500), or by both.

§ 830. Any person who comes within the provisions of this chapter and who otherwise meets all standards imposed by law on a peace officer is a peace officer, and notwithstanding any other provision of law, no person other than those designated in this chapter is a peace officer. The restriction of peace officer functions of any public officer or employee shall not affect his or her status for purposes of retirement.

§ 830.1. (a) Any sheriff, undersheriff, or deputy sheriff, employed in that capacity, of a county, any chief of police of a city or chief, director, or chief executive officer of a consolidated municipal public safety agency that performs police functions, any police officer, employed in that capacity and appointed by the chief of police or chief, director, or chief executive of a public safety agency, of a city, any chief of police, or police officer of a district, including police officers of the San Diego Unified Port District Harbor Police, authorized by statute to maintain a police department, any marshal or deputy marshal of a superior court or county, any port warden or port police officer of the Harbor Department of the City of Los Angeles, or any inspector or investigator employed in that capacity in the office of a district attorney, is a peace officer. The authority of these peace officers extends to any place in the state, as follows:

(1) As to any public offense committed or which there is probable cause to believe has been committed within the political subdivision that employs the peace officer or in which the peace officer serves.

(2) Where the peace officer has the prior consent of the chief of police or chief, director, or chief executive officer of a consolidated municipal public safety agency, or person authorized by him or her to give consent, if the place is within a city or of the sheriff, or person authorized by him or her to give consent, if the place is within a county.

(3) As to any public offense committed or which there is probable cause to believe has been committed in the peace officer's presence, and with respect to which there is immediate danger to person or property, or of the escape of the perpetrator of the offense.

(b) The Attorney General and special agents and investigators of the Department of Justice are peace officers, and those assistant chiefs, deputy chiefs, chiefs, deputy directors, and division directors designated as peace officers by the

Attorney General are peace officers. The authority of these peace officers extends to any place in the state where a public offense has been committed or where there is probable cause to believe one has been committed.

(c) Any deputy sheriff of the County of Los Angeles, and any deputy sheriff of the Counties of Butte, Glenn, Humboldt, Imperial, Inyo, Kern, Kings, Lassen, Mendocino, Plumas, Riverside, San Diego, Santa Barbara, Shasta, Siskiyou, Solano, Sonoma, Stanislaus, Sutter, Tehama, Tulare, and Tuolumne who is employed to perform duties exclusively or initially relating to custodial assignments with responsibilities for maintaining the operations of county custodial facilities, including the custody, care, supervision, security, movement, and transportation of inmates, is a peace officer whose authority extends to any place in the state only while engaged in the performance of the duties of his or her respective employment and for the purpose of carrying out the primary function of employment relating to his or her custodial assignments, or when performing other law enforcement duties directed by his or her employing agency during a local state of emergency.

§ 830.2. The following persons are peace officers whose authority extends to any place in the state:

(a) Any member of the Department of the California Highway Patrol including those members designated under subdivision (a) of Section 2250.1 of the Vehicle Code, provided that the primary duty of the peace officer is the enforcement of any law relating to the use or operation of vehicles upon the highways, or laws pertaining to the provision of police services for the protection of state officers, state properties, and the occupants of state properties, or both, as set forth in the Vehicle Code and Government Code.

(b) A member of the University of California Police Department appointed pursuant to Section 92600 of the Education Code, provided that the primary duty of the peace officer shall be the enforcement of the law within the area specified in Section 92600 of the Education Code.

(c) A member of the California State University Police Departments appointed pursuant to Section 89560 of the Education Code, provided that the primary duty of the peace officer shall be the enforcement of the law within the area specified in Section 89560 of the Education Code.

(d) (1) Any member of the Law Enforcement and Investigations Unit of the Department of Corrections, provided that the primary duties of the peace officer shall be the investigation or apprehension of parolees, parole violators, or escapees from state institutions, the transportation of those persons, and the coordination of those activities with other criminal justice agencies.

(2) Any member of the Office of Internal Affairs of the Department of Corrections, provided that the primary duties shall be criminal investigations of Department of Corrections personnel and the coordination of those activities with other criminal justice agencies. For purposes of this subdivision the member of the Office of Internal Affairs shall possess certification from the Commission on Peace Officer Standards and Training for investigators, or have completed training pursuant to Section 6126.1 of the Penal Code.

(e) Employees of the Department of Fish and Game designated by the director, provided that the primary duty of those peace officers shall be the enforcement of the law as set forth in Section 856 of the Fish and Game Code.

(f) Employees of the Department of Parks and Recreation designated by the director pursuant to Section 5008 of the Public Resources Code, provided that the primary duty of the peace officer shall be the enforcement of the law as set forth in Section 5008 of the Public Resources Code.

(g) The Director of Forestry and Fire Protection and employees or classes of employees of the Department of Forestry and Fire Protection designated by the director pursuant to Section 4156 of the Public Resources Code, provided that the primary duty of the peace officer shall be the enforcement of the law as that duty is set forth in Section 4156 of the Public Resources Code.

(h) Persons employed by the Department of Alcoholic Beverage Control for the enforcement of Division 9 (commencing with Section 23000) of the Business and Professions Code and designated by the Director of Alcoholic Beverage Control, provided that the primary duty of any of these peace officers shall be the enforcement of the laws relating to alcoholic beverages, as that duty is set forth in Section 25755 of the Business and Professions Code.

(i) Marshals and police appointed by the Board of Directors of the California Exposition and State Fair pursuant to Section 3332 of the Food and Agricultural Code, provided that the primary duty of the peace officers shall be the enforcement of the law as prescribed in that section.

(j) The Inspector General, pursuant to Section 6125, and the Chief Deputy Inspector General In Charge, the Senior Deputy Inspector General, the Deputy Inspector General, and those employees of the Inspector General as designated by the Inspector General, are peace officers, provided that the primary duty of these peace officers shall be conducting audits of investigatory practices and other audits, as well as conducting investigations, of the Department of Corrections, the Department of the Youth Authority, the Board of Prison Terms, the Youthful Offender Parole Board, or the Board of Corrections.

§ 830.3. The following persons are peace officers whose authority extends to any place in the state for the purpose of performing their primary duty or when making an arrest pursuant to Section 836 of the Penal Code as to any public offense with respect to which there is immediate danger to person or property, or of the escape of the perpetrator of that offense, or pursuant to Section 8597 or 8598 of the Government Code. These peace officers may carry firearms only if authorized and under those terms and conditions as specified by their employing agencies:

(a) Persons employed by the Division of Investigation of the Department of Consumer Affairs and investigators of the Medical Board of California and the Board of Dental Examiners, who are designated by the Director of Consumer Affairs, provided that the primary duty of these peace officers shall be the enforcement of the law as that duty is set forth in Section 160 of the Business and Professions Code.

(b) Voluntary fire wardens designated by the Director of Forestry and Fire Protection pursuant to Section 4156 of the Public Resources Code, provided that the primary duty of these peace officers shall be the enforcement of the law as that duty is set forth in Section 4156 of that code.

(c) Employees of the Department of Motor Vehicles designated in Section 1655 of the Vehicle Code, provided that the primary duty of these peace officers shall be the enforcement of the law as that duty is set forth in Section 1655 of that code.

(d) Investigators of the California Horse Racing Board designated by the board, provided that the primary duty of these peace officers shall be the enforcement of Chapter 4 (commencing with Section 19400) of Division 8 of the Business and Professions Code and Chapter 10 (commencing with Section 330) of Title 9 of Part 1 of this code.

(e) The State Fire Marshal and assistant or deputy state fire marshals appointed pursuant to Section 13103 of the Health and Safety Code, provided that the primary duty of these peace officers shall be the enforcement of the law as that duty is set forth in Section 13104 of that code.

(f) Inspectors of the food and drug section designated by the chief pursuant to subdivision (a) of Section 106500 of the Health and Safety Code, provided that the primary duty of these peace officers shall be the enforcement of the law as that duty is set forth in Section 106500 of that code.

(g) All investigators of the Division of Labor Standards Enforcement designated by the Labor Commissioner, provided that the primary duty of these peace officers shall be the enforcement of the law as prescribed in Section 95 of the Labor Code.

(h) All investigators of the State Departments of Health Services, Social Services, Mental Health, and Alcohol and Drug Programs, the Department of Toxic Substances Control, the Office of Statewide Health Planning and Development, and the Public Employees' Retirement System, provided that the primary duty of these peace officers shall be the enforcement of the law relating to the duties of his or her department or office. Notwithstanding any other provision of law, investigators of the Public Employees' Retirement System shall not carry firearms.

(i) The Chief of the Bureau of Fraudulent Claims of the Department of Insurance and those investigators designated by the chief, provided that the primary duty of those investigators shall be the enforcement of Section 550.

(j) Employees of the Department of Housing and Community Development designated under Section 18023 of the Health and Safety Code, provided that the primary duty of these peace officers shall be the enforcement of the law as that duty is set forth in Section 18023 of that code.

(k) Investigators of the office of the Controller, provided that the primary duty of these investigators shall be the enforcement of the law relating to the duties of that office. Notwithstanding any other law, except as authorized by the Controller, the peace officers designated pursuant to this subdivision shall not carry firearms.

(l) Investigators of the Department of Corporations designated by the Commissioner of Corporations, provided that the primary duty of these investigators shall be the enforcement of the provisions of law administered by the Department of Corporations. Notwithstanding any other provision of law, the peace officers designated pursuant to this subdivision shall not carry firearms.

(m) Persons employed by the Contractors' State License Board designated by the Director of Consumer Affairs pursuant to Section 7011.5 of the Business and Professions Code, provided that the primary duty of these persons shall be the enforcement of the law as that duty is set forth in Section 7011.5, and in Chapter 9 (commencing with Section 7000) of Division 3, of that code. The Director of Consumer Affairs may designate as peace officers not more than three persons who shall at the time of their designation be assigned to the special investigations unit of the board. Notwithstanding any other provision of law, the persons designated pursuant to this subdivision shall not carry firearms.

(n) The Chief and coordinators of the Law Enforcement Division of the Office of Emergency Services.

(o) Investigators of the office of the Secretary of State designated by the Secretary of State, provided that the primary duty of these peace officers shall be the enforcement of the law as prescribed in Chapter 3 (commencing with Section 8200) of Division 1 of Title 2 of, and Section 12172.5 of, the Government Code. Notwithstanding any other provision of law, the peace officers designated pursuant to this subdivision shall not carry firearms.

(p) The Deputy Director for Security designated by Section 8880.38 of the Government Code, and all lottery security personnel assigned to the California State Lottery and designated by the director, provided that the primary duty of any of those peace officers shall be the enforcement of the laws related to assuring the integrity, honesty, and fairness of the operation and administration of the California State Lottery.

(q) Investigators employed by the Investigation Division of the Employment

Development Department designated by the director of the department, provided that the primary duty of those peace officers shall be the enforcement of the law as that duty is set forth in Section 317 of the Unemployment Insurance Code. Notwithstanding any other provision of law, the peace officers designated pursuant to this subdivision shall not carry firearms.

(r) The chief and assistant chief of museum security and safety of the California Science Center, as designated by the executive director pursuant to Section 4108 of the Food and Agricultural Code, provided that the primary duty of those peace officers shall be the enforcement of the law as that duty is set forth in Section 4108 of the Food and Agricultural Code.

(s) Employees of the Franchise Tax Board designated by the board, provided that the primary duty of these peace officers shall be the enforcement of the law as set forth in Chapter 9 (commencing with Section 19701) of Part 10.2 of Division 2 of the Revenue and Taxation Code.

(t) Notwithstanding any other provision of this section, a peace officer authorized by this section shall not be authorized to carry firearms by his or her employing agency until that agency has adopted a policy on the use of deadly force by those peace officers, and until those peace officers have been instructed in the employing agency's policy on the use of deadly force. Every peace officer authorized pursuant to this section to carry firearms by his or her employing agency shall qualify in the use of the firearms at least every six months.

(u) Investigators of the Department of Managed Health Care designated by the Director of the Department of Managed Health Care, provided that the primary duty of these investigators shall be the enforcement of the provisions of laws administered by the Director of the Department of Managed Health Care. Notwithstanding any other provision of law, the peace officers designated pursuant to this subdivision shall not carry firearms.

(v) The Chief, Deputy Chief, supervising investigators, and investigators of the Office of Protective Services of the State Department of Developmental Services, provided that the primary duty of each of those persons shall be the enforcement of the law relating to the duties of his or her department or office.

Probate Code

§ 4121. A power of attorney is legally sufficient if all of the following requirements are satisfied:

(a) The power of attorney contains the date of its execution.

(b) The power of attorney is signed either (1) by the principal or (2) in the principal's name by some other person in the principal's presence and at the principal's direction.

(c) The power of attorney is either (1) acknowledged before a notary public or (2) signed by at least two witnesses who satisfy the requirements of Section 4122.

§ 4122. If the power of attorney is signed by witnesses, as provided in Section 4121, the following requirements shall be satisfied:

(a) The witnesses shall be adults.

(b) The attorney-in-fact may not act as a witness.

(c) Each witness signing the power of attorney shall witness either the signing of the instrument by the principal or the principal's acknowledgment of the signature or the power of attorney.

(d) In the case of a durable power of attorney for health care, the additional requirements of Section 4701.

§ 4307. (a) A copy of a power of attorney certified under this section has the same force and effect as the original power of attorney.

(b) A copy of a power of attorney may be certified by any of the following:

(1) An attorney authorized to practice law in this state.

(2) A notary public in this state.

(3) An official of a state or of a political subdivision who is authorized to make certifications.

(c) The certification shall state that the certifying person has examined the original power of attorney and the copy and that the copy is a true and correct copy of the original power of attorney.

(d) Nothing in this section is intended to create an implication that a third person may be liable for acting in good faith reliance on a copy of a power of attorney that has not been certified under this section.

§ 4673. (a) A written advance health care directive is legally sufficient if all of the following requirements are satisfied:

(1) The advance directive contains the date of its execution.

(2) The advance directive is signed either by the patient or in the patient's name by another adult in the patient's presence and at the patient's direction.

(3) The advance directive is either acknowledged before a notary public or signed by at least two witnesses who satisfy the requirements of Sections 4674 and 4675. (b) An electronic advance health care directive or power of attorney for health care is legally sufficient if the requirements in subdivision (a) are satisfied, except that for the purposes of paragraph (3) of subdivision (a), an acknowledgment before a notary public shall be required, and if a digital signature is used, it meets all of the following requirements:

(1) The digital signature either meets the requirements of Section 16.5 of the Government Code and Chapter 10 (commencing with Section 22000) of Division 7 of Title 2 of the California Code of Regulations or the digital signature uses an algorithm approved by the National Institute of Standards and Technology.

(2) The digital signature is unique to the person using it.

(3) The digital signature is capable of verification.

(4) The digital signature is under the sole control of the person using it.

(5) The digital signature is linked to data in such a manner that if the data are changed, the digital signature is invalidated.

(6) The digital signature persists with the document and not by association in separate files.

(7) The digital signature is bound to a digital certificate.

§ 4701. If the durable power of attorney for health care is signed by witnesses, as provided in Section 4121, in addition to the requirements applicable to witnesses under Section 4122, the following requirements shall be satisfied: ***

(e) If the principal is a patient in a skilled nursing facility, as defined in subdivision (c) of Section 1250 of the Health and Safety Code, at the time the durable power of attorney for health care is executed, the power of attorney is not effective unless a patient advocate or ombudsman as may be designated by the Department of Aging for this purpose pursuant to any other applicable provision of law signs the instrument as a witness, either as one of two witnesses or in addition to notarization pursuant to subdivision (c) of Section 4121. The patient advocate or ombudsman shall declare that he or she is serving as a witness as required by this subdivision. It is the intent of this subdivision to recognize that some patients in skilled nursing facilities are insulated from a voluntary decision-making role, by virtue of the custodial nature of their care, so as to require special assurance that they are capable of willfully and voluntarily executing a durable power of attorney for health care.

Health and Safety Code

§ 103526. (a) A faxed notary acknowledgment accompanying a faxed request received pursuant to this subdivision for a certified copy of a birth or death record or a military service record shall be legible and, if the notary's seal is not photographically reproducible, show the name of the notary, the county of the notary's principal place of business, the notary's telephone number, the notary's registration number, and the notary's commission expiration date typed or printed in a manner that is photographically reproducible below, or immediately adjacent to, the notary's signature in the acknowledgment.

Uniform Commercial Code

§ 3505.***

(b) A protest is a certificate of dishonor made by a United States consul or vice consul, or a notary public or other person authorized to administer oaths by the law of the place where dishonor occurs. It may be made upon information satisfactory to that person. The protest shall identify the instrument and certify either that presentment has been made or, if not made, the reason why it was not made, and that the instrument has been dishonored by nonacceptance or nonpayment. The protest may also certify that notice of dishonor has been given to some or all parties.

Los Angeles County Code

2.32.202 **Notary journal surrender fee.** The Registrar-Recorder/County Clerk shall charge a fee of $10 for processing surrendered notary journals.

2.32.204 **Notary manual replacement fee.** The Registrar-Recorder/County Clerk shall charge a fee of $40 for a replacement notary manual.

FEDERAL STATUTES

United States Code

§ 936. Art. 136. **Authority to administer oaths and to act as notary**

(a) The following persons on active duty or performing inactive-duty training may administer oaths for the purposes of military administration, including military justice:

(1) All judge advocates.

(2) All summary courts-martial.

(3) All adjutants, assistant adjutants, acting adjutants, and personnel adjutants.

(4) All commanding officers of the Navy, Marine Corps, and Coast Guard.

(5) All staff judge advocates and legal officers, and acting or assistant staff judge advocates and legal officers.

(6) All other persons designated by regulations of the armed forces or by statute.

(b) The following persons on active duty or performing inactive-duty training may administer oaths necessary in the performance of their duties:

(1) The president, military judge, trial counsel, and assistant trial counsel for all general and special courts-martial.

(2) The president and the counsel for the court of any court of inquiry.

(3) All officers designated to take a deposition.

(4) All persons detailed to conduct an investigation.

(5) All recruiting officers.

(6) All other persons designated by regulations of the armed forces or by statute.

§ 1044a. Authority to act as notary

(a) The persons named in subsection (b) have the general powers of a notary public and of a consul of the United States in the performance of all notarial acts to be executed by any of the following:

(1) Members of any of the armed forces.

(2) Other persons eligible for legal assistance under the provisions of section 1044 of this title or regulations of the Department of Defense.

(3) Persons serving with, employed by, or accompanying the armed forces outside the United States and outside the Commonwealth of Puerto Rico, Guam, and the Virgin Islands.

(4) Other persons subject to the Uniform Code of Military Justice (chapter 47 of this title) outside the United States.

(b) Persons with the powers described in subsection (a) are the following:

(1) All judge advocates, including reserve judge advocates when not in a duty status.

(2) All civilian attorneys serving as legal assistance attorneys.

(3) All adjutants, assistant adjutants, and personnel adjutants, including reserve members when not in a duty status.

(4) All other members of the armed forces, including reserve members when not in a duty status, who are designated by regulations of the armed forces or by statute to have those powers.

(5) For the performance of notarial acts at locations outside the United States, all employees of a military department or the Coast Guard who are designated by regulations of the Secretary concerned or by statute to have those powers for exercise outside the United States.

(c) No fee may be paid to or received by any person for the performance of a notarial act authorized in this section.

(d) The signature of any such person acting as notary, together with the title of that person's offices, is prima facie evidence that the signature is genuine, that the person holds the designated title, and that the person is authorized to perform a notarial act. ■

Documents Affecting Real Property

Below is a list of documents that may be utilized in California that affect real property and, therefore, would require securing a journal thumbprint of the signer. In addition, Notaries may not perform proofs of execution on any of these documents. This list is not meant to be exhaustive.

Real Property Documents
- Affidavit to Affirm Conveyance
- Affidavit of Continuous Marriage
- Affidavit of Death of Spouse
- Affidavit of Death of Spouse — Community Property With Rights of Survivorship
- Affidavit of Death of Joint Tenant
- Affidavit (Grantor)
- Affidavit of No Debts/Liens
- Affidavit of Settlement Agent
- Affidavit of Surviving Spouse Succeeding to Title to Community Property by Right of Survivorship
- Affidavit of Uninsured Deed
- All-Inclusive Note Secured by Deed of Trust
- Assignment — General
- Assignment of Deed of Trust and Request for Special Notice
- Assignment of Deed of Trust
- Assignment of Mortgage
- Assignment of Ownership Documents
- Assignment of Proprietary Lease
- Certification of Trust
- Claim of Lien
- Corporation Assignment of Deed of Trust

DOCUMENTS AFFECTING REAL PROPERTY

- Declaration of Abandonment of Declared Homestead
- Declaration/Uninsured Deed
- Declaration of Trust
- Estoppel Affidavit (by Individual Giving in Lieu of Foreclosure)
- Full Reconveyance
- Grant Deed (Trust Transfer)
- Homestead Declaration
- Homestead Declaration (Spouses and Declared Owners)
- Homestead Waiver
- Memorandum of Option
- Modification and Supplement to Deed of Trust
- Long Form Security Land Contract (Installment)
- Long Form All-Inclusive Deed of Trust and Assignment of Rents
- Long Form Deed of Trust and Assignment of Rents
- Notice of Rescission of Declaration of Default and Demand for Sale and of Notice of Default and Election to Sell under Deed of Trust
- Notice of Default
- Notice of Non-Responsibility
- Notice of Termination of Right of First Refusal
- Partial Reconveyance
- Rescission of Trustee's Deed
- Release of Abstract
- Release of Claim of Mortgage Lien
- Release of Mortgage
- Release of Mechanic's Lien
- Request for Conveyance
- Request for Full Reconveyance
- Request for Notice
- Request for Partial Reconveyance
- Revocation of Power of Attorney
- Satisfaction of Mortgage
- Seller's Affidavit
- Short Form Deed of Trust and Assignment of Rents (Individual)
- Specific Release of Lien
- Subordination Agreement
- Subordination Agreement — Existing Deed of Trust to New Deed of Trust
- Subordination Agreement — New Deed of Trust to New Deed of Trust

- Subordination Agreement — Existing Deed of Trust to Additional Advance
- Subordination Agreement — Lease to Deed of Trust
- Substitution of Trustee
- Substitution of Trustee and Full Reconveyance
- Trust Certificate
- Trustee's Deed Upon Sale

Deeds
- Corporate Quitclaim Deed
- Grant Deed
- Quitclaim Deed
- Interspousal Grant Deed
- Interspousal Transfer Grant Deed
- Joint Tenancy Deed
- Trust Transfer Grant Deed

Loan Documents
- Address Certification
- Affidavit and Indemnity
- Affidavit of Common Identity
- Affidavit of Identity
- Affidavit of Income/Credit/Employment
- Affidavit of Occupancy
- Affidavit of Payment of Taxes
- Affidavit of Title
- AKA Statement
- Assignment of Rents
- Assumptor Affidavit
- Borrower Certifications
- Borrower's Loan Affidavit
- Closing Affidavit
- Compliance Agreement
- Correction Agreement
- Deed of Trust
- Deed of Trust and Fixture Filing
- Document Execution and Re-Execution Agreement
- Error and Omissions Compliance Agreement
- Homeowner's Policy of Title Insurance Affidavit
- Identification Affidavit
- Identity Certificate/Name Affidavit
- Mortgagor's Affidavit

DOCUMENTS AFFECTING REAL PROPERTY

- Name Affidavit
- Name/AKA Affidavit
- Name Affidavit (One and the Same Certification)
- Signature Affidavit
- Signature Affidavit and AKA Statement
- Signature Certificate/Affidavit
- Signature Certification
- Survey Affidavit
- Occupancy Affidavit and Financial Status
- Occupancy, Misrepresentation, Non-disclosure Affidavit and Agreement
- One and the Same Affidavit
- Owner Occupancy Affidavit

Powers of Attorney
- Power of Attorney
- Limited Power of Attorney
- Special Power of Attorney
- Correction Agreement Limited Power of Attorney

About the NNA

Since 1957, the National Notary Association has been committed to serving and educating the nation's Notaries. During that time, the NNA® has become known as the most trusted source of information for and about Notaries and Notary laws, rules and best practices.

The NNA serves Notaries through its NationalNotary.org website, social media, publications, annual conferences, seminars, online training and the NNA® Hotline, which offers immediate answers to specific questions about notarization.

In addition, the NNA offers the highest quality professional supplies, including official seals and stamps, recordkeeping journals, Notary certificates and Notary bonds.

Though dedicated primarily to educating and assisting Notaries, the NNA supports implementing effective Notary laws and informing the public about the Notary's vital role in today's society.

To learn more about the National Notary Association visit *www.NationalNotary.org.* ■

Index

A

Acknowledgment....... 10, **12–16**, 37, 40, 44, 46, 63, 65
   Certificate **13–15**, 37
   Failure to complete............**14**, 63
   False certificate **14**, 40, 63, 65
   Fee...44
   Forged or counterfeited............65
   Identification ... 12, 14, 23, **26–28**
   Incomplete document 46
   Notice 13
   Out-of-state 13–15
   Perjury, taken under penalty
      of..13
   Personal appearance **12**, 14
   Purpose 10, **12**
   Signature, in Notary's
      presence 12, **14**
   Terminology................................ 5
   Who may take.....................15–16
Address, change of....................**9**, 10
Advertising.................. **52–53**, 54, 61
   False or misleading............**52**, 61
   Foreign-language **52–54**, 61–62
   Immigration consultant.....**53**, 54, 62
Affidavit **17–18**, 20
Affirmation. *See* Oath or affirmation
Apostille. *See* Authentication

Application, commission.
   See Commission, Notary
Authentication..........................50–52
Awareness, determining.......... 26, 54

B

Beneficial interest. *See* Disqualifying interest
Birth certificate. *See* Public record
Bond, Notary **5–6**, 8, 9, 10, 67
   Address-change requirement ... 9, 10
   Filing..**5**, 8
   Liability 6, 67
   Name-change requirement.......10
   Protects public 5–6
   Public-employee Notary............ 8
   Requirement......................**5–6**, 8
   Surety....................................... 5, 6
   Surety's release........................... 6

C

Cancellation, commission.
   See Commission, Notary
Certificate, Notary. 14, **37–39**, 63, 68
   Acknowledgment........ **13–15**, 37
   Affidavit 17
   Certified copy of journal
      entry...16

Page numbers listed in **bold** indicate where the most complete information on a subject can be found.

Certified copy of power of
    attorney..................................16
Contents 37–38
Deposition................................18
False (or writing) ...14, **40**, 63, 68
Foreign-language 53
Form 38–39
Jurat **19**, 37
Marriage, confidential...............58
Military-base Notary..................56
Pre-sign/pre-seal 39–40
Proof of execution 22–23
Protest......................................25
Requirement............................37
Signature-by-mark.....................49
Signature requirement,
    Notary's..................................38
Size requirement for
    recording 40
SS, SCT (*scilicet*) 37
Statement of particulars............37
Testimonium clause 37–38
Venue................................19, **37**
Certificate of Authorization to
    Manufacture Seal. *See* Seal,
    Notary
Certified copy of journal entry.
    See Copy of journal entry
Certified copy of power of
    attorney.............. 11, **16–17**, 44
    Certificate 16
    Fee..44
    Identification 16
    Journal entry 16
    Procedure...................................16
    Purpose 11
Certified copy, unauthorized ...11–12
Change of address. *See* Address,
    change of
Change of name. *See* Name, change
    of
Check, dishonored. *See* Misconduct
Child-support payment delinquency.
    See Misconduct
Citizenship. *See* Commission, Notary
Commission, Notary.....**2–10**, 36–37,
    60–68
    Amended..............................9–10

Application...................**2–4**, 9, 66
Application misstatement.....**3–4**,
    60–61
Bond................. **5–6**, 8, 9, 10, 67
Cancellation.........................**4**, 66
Certificate of Authorization to
    manufacture seal......**42**, 43, 66
Citizenship.................................. 3
Death of Notary 8, **36–37**
Denial.. 14, 20, 22, 30, 40, 43, 45,
    60–67, 68
Education 4, 7, 55
Employee-Notary **34–35**, 48
Exam.................................4, 7, 55
Expiration 4, **7**, 68
Fees **3**, 4, 5, 7, 9, 66
Fingerprints 3, **4–5**
Jurisdiction **7**, 55–56
Military-base Notary............55–56
Oath of office...........**6–7**, 8, 9, 10
Public-employee Notary..**8–9**, 45
Qualifications 2–3
Reappointment......................7–8
Residency requirement............. 3
Resignation.....................**8**, 37, 68
Revocation... 6, 14, 20, 22, 30, 36,
    39, 43, 45, 53–54, 54, **60–68**, 68
Seal purchase 8, 9, 10, **42**, 43
Suspension 14, 20, 22, 35, 40,
    43, 45, 53, 54, **60–67**, 68
Term of office 7, 8, 55
Communication, Notary/signer.....21,
    53
Confidential marriage. *See* Marriage
    certificate, confidential
Copy certification. *See* Certified
    copy
Copy of journal entry.............10, **16**,
    34–35, 44
    Certificate 17
    Certified....................11, **16**, 35
    Court order................................16
    Employer request............. **34–35**
    Fee..44
    Public request **34**, 44
    Secretary of State request..16, **35**
    Subpoena 16

INDEX

Credible identifying witness .. 21, 23, 26, **28–30**, 50, 65
   Acknowledgment, for **26**
   Identification, failure to
      obtain 65
   Identification of 28
   Journal entry 30
   Jurat, for 26
   Minor signer, for 50
   Oath or affirmation 21, **29–30**
   Purpose 28
   Qualifications 28
   Subscribing witness, confusion
      with 30
   Subscribing witness, for 22
Criminal conviction. *See* Misconduct
Customers, restricting service to.
   See Employer/Notary agreement

D

Date of document. *See* Document(s)
Death certificate. *See* Public record
Death of Notary. *See* Commission, Notary
Denial, commission.
   See Commission, Notary
Deposition 11, **16–17**, 44
Digital signature. *See* Signature, Notary's
Disqualifying interest 46–47
Document(s)
   Foreign-language, notarizing ... 53
   Immigration 44, **54**, 65–66
   Incomplete 46
   Preparation 52
   Real property (thumbprint
      requirement) 33–34
Durable power of attorney for
   healthcare. *See* Power of
   attorney for health care, durable
Duty, failure of. *See* Misconduct

E

Education, Notary. *See* Commission, Notary

Education-provider violation.
   See Misconduct
Electronic seal. *See* Seal, Notary
Electronic signature. *See* Signature, Notary's
Embossing seal. *See* Seal, Notary
Employee-Notary. *See* Commission, Notary
Employer/Notary agreement .. **48–49**
Errors and omissions insurance 6
Exam, Notary. *See* Commission, Notary
Expiration, commission.
   See Commission, Notary

F

Faxes 46
Fee(s) . **3**, 5, 7, 36, **44–45**, 46, 59, 62
   Absentee ballot 46
   Acknowledgment 44
   Advertising, in foreign-
      language **52**, 61
   Authentication 50–51
   Certified copy of power of
      attorney 44
   Commission application **3**, 4,
      7, 9, 66
   Copy of journal entry 44
   Deposition 44
   Employee-Notary **48**
   Filing, oath and bond 5, 7, 9
   Fingerprint **3**, **5**
   Immigration documents **44**, 62
   Itemize, obligation or refusal
      to 45
   Journal surrender (county
      clerk) 36
   Jurat 45
   Marriage certificate,
      confidential 58
   Maximum notarial 31, **44–45**
   Military-base Notary 55
   Oath or affirmation 45
   Option not to charge 45
   Overcharging **45**, 62

Page numbers listed in **bold** indicate where the most complete information on a subject can be found.

Proof of execution.....................45
Public-employee Notary......**9**, 45
Recording (non-standard size certificate)..............................40
Travel...45
Felony conviction. *See* Misconduct
Financial interest. *See* Disqualifying interest
Fingerprints. *See* Commission, Notary
Foreign-language.............. **52–53**, 61
   Advertising.................. **52–53**, 61
   Certificate 53
   Document, notarizing...............53
   Signature, notarizing..................54
   Signer..54
Fraud. *See* Misconduct

G

Grand theft. *See* Misconduct

H

Hearing, right to. *See* Misconduct
Homeowner's association election.......................................59

I

Identification............... 12, 14, 16, 19, **26–30**, 50, 54, 65
   Acknowledgment, for.......12, **14**, 23, **27–29**
   Certified-copy-requester...........16
   Credible-identifying-witness.....28
   Credible-identifying-witness, failure to obtain......................65
   Credible identifying witness, using. *See* Credible identifying witness
   Documents, using. *See* Identification document
   Immigration-document-signer 54
   Jurat, for 19, **26–28**
   Minor-signer 50
   Personal knowledge, using......26
   Representative-signer.........14, **26**
   Satisfactory evidence, using 12, 14, 19, **26**, 50

Subscribing-witness **23**, 26
Identification document......... **26–28**
   Acceptable...........................27–29
   Acknowledgment, for. 14, **26–28**
   Credible identifying witness, for...28
   Jurat, for 26–28
   Minor signer, for 50
   Multiple 28
   Unacceptable 28
Immigration consultant ... 44, **54–55**, 62–63
   Advertising **53**, 54, 61
   Fee...**44**, 62
   Unbonded 53–54, **62–63**
Immigration document.... 44, **54–55**, 65–66
   Completing or notarizing ...54–55
   False statement on....... **54**, 65–66
   Fee for completing **44**, 62
   Identification of signer 54
   Naturalization certificate...........54
Impersonating a Notary. *See* Misconduct
Incomplete document. *See* Document(s)
Influence, unlawful. *See* Misconduct
Inking seal. *See* Seal, Notary
Insurance, errors and omissions. *See* Errors and omissions insurance

J

Journal of notarial acts 7, 11, 17, **30–36**, 44, 64, 65, 67–68, 68
   Access, failure to provide..**35**, 64
   Certified-copy-of-power-of-attorney entry 16
   Court order.................................16
   Credible-identifying-witness entry...30
   Deliver, refusal to **37**, 65
   Destroyed, defaced or concealed **37**, 68
   Disposition 8, **37–38**
   Employer request.............. **34–35**
   Entries...................................30–33

Entry, certified copy of.....11, **16**, 35
Fee for copy of entry................44
Fee for surrender to county clerk........................36
Law-enforcement access.....35–36
Loss or theft, failure to report..64
Lost or stolen 35
Maintain, failure to....... **30**, 67–68
Public request **34**, 44
Requirement..............................30
Secretary of State request..16, **35**
Secure, failure to................**30**, 65
Security......................................35
Subpoena 16
Subscribing-witness entry.........31
Surrender, unauthorized...........35
Thumbprint, failure to obtain......................**34**, 65, 68
Thumbprint requirement...22–23, **33–35**, 57, 58
Judgment, non-payment of.
  See Misconduct
Jurat...................... 11, **18–20**, 37, 45
Age of signer, verifying 19–20
Certificate **19**, 37
Fee...45
Identification 19, **26–28**
Notice 19
Oath or affirmation...................19
Oath or affirmation, failure to administer.................20, **22**, 65
Personal appearance 18
Purpose 11, **18–19**
Signature, in Notary's presence 18
Venue, location of.....................19
Jurisdiction. *See* Commission, Notary

L

Law, unauthorized practice of **52**, 56, 62
Liability protection................6, 48–49
Living will. *See* Will

Loose certificate. *See* Certificate, Notary
L.S. (*locus sigilli*). *See* Certificate, Notary

M

Map, plastic subdivision. *See* Seal, Notary
Marriage ceremony........................59
Marriage certificate, confidential....58
Military-base Notary.
  See Commission, Notary
Military-personnel notarization 56–57
Minor signer, notarizing for 50
Misconduct
Acknowledgment certificate, false.....................14, 40, **63**, 65
Acknowledgment, failure to complete.........................14, **63**
Acknowledgment, forged or counterfeited 65
Address change, failure to notify Secretary of State.................... 9
Advertising, false or misleading 52, **61**
Advertising, improper foreign-language 52–53, **61**
Advertising, improper immigration consultant ..54, **62**
Application misstatement 3–4, **60–61**
Cancellation, commission.
  See Commission, Notary
Certificate or writing, false 14, 40, **63**, 68
Check, dishonored...............4, **66**
Child-support payment delinquency......................4, **66**
Commission cancellation.
  See Commission, Notary
Commission denial.
  See Commission, Notary
Commission resignation.
  See Commission, Notary

Page numbers listed in **bold** indicate where the most complete information on a subject can be found.

119

Commission revocation.
See Commission, Notary
Commission suspension.
See Commission, Notary
Credible identifying witness, failure to obtain ID for..........65
Criminal conviction............60, **67**
Denial, commission.
See Commission, Notary
Dishonesty..........................61, **62**
Duty, failure of..........................60
Education-provider violation....66
Fees, overcharging..............45, **62**
Fees, refusal to itemize..............45
Felony conviction **60**, 67
Fraud **62**, 63
Grand theft................................64
Hearing, right to........................68
ID for credible identifying witness, failure to obtain 65
Immigration consultant, unbonded...........54–55, **62–63**
Immigration document, false statement on............ 54, **65–66**
Impersonating a Notary............61
Influence, unlawful..............**64**, 68
Investigation............................68
Journal access, failure to provide 35, **64**
Journal destroyed, defaced or concealed **37**, 68
Journal, failure to maintain 30, **67–68**
Journal, failure to secure...35, **65**
Journal loss or theft, failure to report 64
Journal, refusal to deliver..37, **65**
Journal surrender, unauthorized 35
Journal thumbprint, failure to obtain........................34, **65**, 68
Judgment, non-payment of 66
Law, unauthorized practice of..........................52, 56, **62**
Name change, failure to notify Secretary of State...................10
Naturalization certificate, copy of..54

Notario publico, use of......53–54, **61**
Notarization, failure to complete after fee paid........... **46–47**, 48
Oath or affirmation, failure to administer.................20, 22, **65**
Personal information, misuse of 64
Professional misconduct...........60
Recording false instrument......................63–64
Refusal of service......... **46–47**, 47
Resignation, commission.
See Commission, Notary
Revocation, commission.
See Commission, Notary
Seal control, failure to keep................................67–68
Seal, failure to secure 43, **65**, 67–68
Seal, forged or counterfeited...43, **65**
Seal loss or damage, failure to report 43, **66–67**
Seal manufacturing procedure, failure to comply with ...42, **66**
Seal surrender, unauthorized ..43, **67–68**
Seal use in endorsement ...43, **66**
Signature, forged or counterfeited (Notary's)........65
Signature, notarizing own .52, **60**
Statement of material fact, false..................................40, **63**
Statement to Notary, false ..61–62
Statute of limitations...........67–68
Suspension, commission.
See Commission, Notary

N

Name, change of 9–10
Naturalization certificate.
See Misconduct
Notarial act(s) **10–25**, 37, 44–45
 Acknowledgment. 10, **12–16**, 37, 40, 44, 46, 63, 65
 Affidavit...................... **17–18**, 20
 Authorized, list of 10–11

Certified copy of journal entry............................10, **16**, 35
Certified copy of power of attorney............... 11, **16–17**, 44
Deposition.............. 11, **16–17**, 44
Failure to complete after fee paid............................ **46–47**, 48
Jurat.................. 11, **18–20**, 37, 45
Oath or affirmation............ 11, 18, **20–22**, 23, 29–30, 45, 65
Proof of execution........11, 15–16, 21, **22–24**, 26, 31, 45, 46
Protest............................ 11, **24–25**
Unauthorized **11–12**, 59

Notario publico. See Misconduct

O

Oath of office, Notary ...**6–7**, 8, 9, 10
   Address-change requirement 9
   Filing..................................**6–7**, 8
   Name-change requirement.......10
   Requirement.......................**6–7**, 8
Oath or affirmation.... 11, 18, **19–21**, 23, 29–30, 45, 65
   Affidavit...............................**18**, 20
   Ceremony and gestures............21
   Credible identifying witness....21, **29–30**
   Deposition..................................18
   Failure to administer....20, **22**, 65
   Fee..45
   Jurat..19
   Perjury, taken under penalty of..20
   Power to administer 20
   Purpose 11, **20**
   Response required...... 18, **21–22**
   Subscribing witness 21, **23**
   Witness in court.........................20
   Wording...............................20–21

P

Personal appearance.............. 12, 14, 18, 22, 25
Personal information, misuse of. *See* Misconduct
Personal knowledge of identity. *See* Identification
Photocopies 46
Power of attorney, certified copy of. *See* Certified copy of power of attorney
Power of attorney for health care, durable 56–58
Practice of law, unauthorized. *See* Law, unauthorized practice of
Proof of execution by subscribing witness...... 11, 15–16, 21, **22–24**, 26, 31, 45, 46
   Certificate 23–24
   Fee..45
   Identification **23**, 26
   Incomplete document 46
   In lieu of acknowledgment....**22**, 23
   Journal entry 33
   Limitations...........................22–23
   Notice 23
   Oath or affirmation............21, **23**
   Personal appearance 22
   Purpose 11, **22**
   Subscribing witness **22**, 30
   Who may take.....................15–16
   Witness jurat.............................22
Protest 11, **24–25**
Public-employee Notary. *See* Commission, Notary
Public record 11

Q

Qualifications. *See* Commission, Notary

R

Reappointment, commission. *See* Commission, Notary
Reasonable care........................48–49

Page numbers listed in **bold** indicate where the most complete information on a subject can be found.

Recordable document. *See* Public record
Recording false instrument. *See* Misconduct
Record, notarial. *See* Journal of notarial acts
Refusal of service.........46–47, **48–49**
 Misconduct............ **45–46**, 47, 48
Relative, notarizing for. *See* Family member, notarizing for
Representative signer 14, **26**
Residency requirement.
 See Commission, Notary
Resignation, commission.
 See Commission, Notary
Revocation, commission.
 See Commission, Notary

S

Satisfactory evidence.
 See Identification
Seal, Notary..............8, 9, 10, **40–44**, 59, 65–67, 68
 Address-change requirement 9
 Certificate of Authorization to Manufacture..............**42**, 43, 66
 Control, failure to keep 67–68
 Disposal..................**8**, 67
 Electronic.................... **44–45**, 59
 Forged or counterfeited.....**43**, 65
 Format 40
 Illegible........................42
 Inking **40**
 Loss or damage, failure to report **43**, 66–67
 Lost or damaged 43
 L.S. (*locus sigilli*)......................41
 Manufacturing procedure, failure to comply with................**42**, 66
 Map, on plastic subdivision 42
 Name-change requirement.......10
 Placement....................41
 Purchase 8, 9, 10, **42**
 Recording requirement..............42
 Required information................41
 Requirement.......................40
 Secure, failure to....**43**, 65, 67–68
 Security 43–44

Surrender, unauthorized..........**43**, 67–68
 Use in endorsement...........**43**, 66
Self-notarization. *See* Signature, Notary's
Signature by mark 49
Signature, Notary's
 Electronic or digital..... 44, **57–59**
 Forged or counterfeited............65
 Notarizing own 52, **60**
 Requirement............................38
Signature, signer's
 Electronic or digital..... **57–59**, 59
 Foreign-language 54
 In Notary's presence....12, **14**, 18
 Minor signer 50
SS, SCT (*scilicet*). *See* Venue
Statement of material fact, false.
 See Misconduct
Statement of particulars.
 See Certificate, Notary
Statement to Notary, false.
 See Misconduct
Statute of limitations.................67–68
Subscribing witness. *See* Proof of execution
Suspension, commission.
 See Commission, Notary

T

Term of office. *See* Commission, Notary
Testimonium clause. *See* Certificate, Notary
Thumbprint....................... **33–35**, 65
 Documents affecting real property, for 33–34
 Failure to obtain...........**34**, 65, 68
 Requirement..........22–23, **33–35**, 56, 58

U

Unauthorized practice of law.
 See Law, unauthorized practice of
Uniform Electronic Transactions Act (UETA)........................59

V

Venue 19, **37**
    Definition **37**
    Jurat, location of 19
    SS, SCT (*scilicet*) 37
Vital record. *See* Public record

W

Will 56–57
    Living 56
Willingness, determining......... 25, 54
Witness jurat. *See* Proof of execution
Wording, notarial. *See* Certificate,
    Notary

Page numbers listed in **bold** indicate where the most complete information on a subject can be found.

NOTES